Level F

Finish Line
Math

Continental Press
Elizabethtown, PA 17022

Credits

Writers: David Herzog and Katherine Mowery

Editors: K. E. Possler and Megan Bergonzi

Cover Design: Mike Reilly

Interior Design: Earl Cummins

Consultants: Robert Gyles, C.S.D 4, New York, New York
Fred Remer, C.S.D. 9, Bronx, New York

Photo Credits: **PhotoDisc, Inc.:** front cover and title page, *students and a teacher;* **Corbis Stock Market, Inc.:** front cover and title page, *hand holding pencil, stop watch, race*

ISBN 0-8454-9281-0

Contents

Introduction

About This Book

Finish Line Math will help you get ready to take mathematics tests. This book contains lessons to review the things you have learned in math class. After each lesson, several pages of problems help you practice what you have reviewed.

The practice pages have three kinds of problems. That's because math tests sometimes have more than one kind of question. The questions will help you find out what you know about math ideas, skills, and problem solving. Like the items on math tests, some problems are very easy. Others may make you think a bit. And a few will be a challenge.

The first practice page has multiple-choice problems. These problems give you four answers to pick from. The first problem is always a sample. A box under the sample tells you how to find the answer.

The second page has short writing problems. These problems ask you to show your work. You may need to demonstrate that you know how to add, subtract, multiply, or divide. You may have to draw and label a diagram. You may need to write a short answer. Again, the first problem on this page is a sample. The answer to it is explained.

The last practice page has one writing problem. This one is longer and often has more than one part. The first part may ask you to solve a problem and show your work. The second part usually asks you to explain what steps you took or why you think your answer is correct. This item has hints to point you in the right direction.

At the end of each unit, you'll find two pages of problems that review all the lessons in that unit.

A practice test for all the units appears at the very end of the book. All the different math topics are mixed up here. The practice test lets you try out what you've learned before you take the real test.

Remember—

To solve a problem—
- Read it carefully. Be sure you know **what** it is asking for.
- Plan how to find the answer.
- Carry out your plan.
- Check your work.

Be sure you read **all** the answer choices. Some may be tricky.

To answer a writing question—
- Follow the item directions exactly.
- Show **all** your work if the item tells you to.
- Label your answer.

Always think about what you will say **before** writing an explanation. Explain your thoughts clearly. Write them neatly.

Test-Taking Tips

When you take a test, you want to do your best. Here are some things you can do to make sure you are in top form.

Remember—

- ◎ **Get enough sleep.** You need to feel rested to be alert. So go to bed early the night before a test.

  Most students need 8 hours of sleep every night.

- ◎ **Eat a good breakfast.** Food gives you the energy you need to think clearly. And you want to think about the test, not about food.

- ◎ **Have everything you need.** Check that you have two sharp pencils with good erasers. Bring any special tools, such as a ruler or a calculator, your teacher says to bring.

  Do you wear glasses? Don't forget them!

- ◎ **Follow all directions.** Listen carefully to the test directions so that you know exactly what to do. If you don't understand any part of them, ask your teacher to explain them again before the test begins.

- ◎ **Check the answer sheet.** Make sure the answer you are marking on the answer sheet has the same number as the problem you are working on. Fill in answer spaces completely. If you erase, do it carefully and completely.

  Compare the number of the problem to the number on the answer sheet often.

- ◎ **Concentrate.** Pay attention to what you are doing. Do not be concerned about what page others are on.

- ◎ **Pace yourself.** Your teacher will tell you how many problems there are and how much time you have to solve them. Don't spend too much time on any one item. You can always skip it and go back to it later.

  Try to allow enough time to go back and check your work.

- ◎ **Be confident.** You have prepared all year for the tests you take. You have learned a lot. So use this chance to show what you know. You may not be sure of all the answers, but use your *best* thinking. That is all anyone expects.

Good Luck!

1–1 Whole Numbers

✳ **Compare** whole numbers by comparing the digits in the same places, starting on the left.

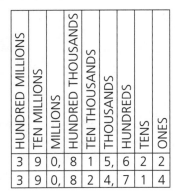

Both numbers have the same digits in the hundred millions, ten millions, millions, and hundred thousands places. The first digits that are different are in the ten thousands place. The first number has a 1 and the second number has a 2, and 1 ten thousand is less than 2 ten thousands. So 390,815,622 is less than 390,824,714.

$$390{,}815{,}622 < 390{,}824{,}714$$

✳ To **round** a number to a certain place value, look at the digit in the **next** place to the right. If the digit is 4 or less, round down. If the digit is 5 or more, round up.

To round to the nearest thousand, look at the hundreds digit.

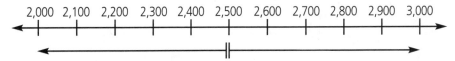

2,498 rounds down to 2,000.

2,501 rounds up to 3,000.

Remember—

There are several ways to name numbers:

- **standard form**

    6,152

- **word form**

    six thousand, one hundred fifty-two

- **expanded form**

    6,000 + 100 + 50 + 2

    or

    $(6 \times 1{,}000) + (1 \times 100) + (5 \times 10) + (2 \times 1)$

The value of a digit depends on its **place value.** The value of each place is ten times the value of the place to its right.

The symbol $>$ means *is greater than.* The symbol $<$ means *is less than.* The symbol always points to the smaller number.

Read each problem. Circle the letter of the best answer.

1 What temperature does the thermometer show?

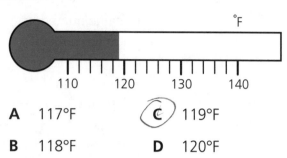

A 117°F   **C** 119°F

B 118°F   **D** 120°F

> Did you select C? That's right. Each tick mark between the numbers stands for 2°. Count by 2s to 118°. The temperature is shown halfway between 118° and 120°. That's 119°.

2 The Earth's orbit about the sun is about 186 million miles in diameter. Which of these is another way to write 186 million?

F 1,860,000   **H** 186,000,000

G 18,600,000   **J** 1,860,000,000

3 Alexei wrote down the total attendance for the classic car show as 48,567 people. By accident, he switched the hundreds and ten thousands digits. What was the correct number of people at the show?

A 45,867   **C** 58,467

B 54,867   **D** 84,567

4 Which of these shows 8,305 written in expanded notation?

F (8 × 1,000) + (3 × 100) + (5 × 1)

G (80 × 1,000) + (3 × 10) + (5 × 1)

H (8 × 1,000) + (3 × 100) + (5 × 10)

J (8 × 1,000) + (3 × 1,000) + (5 × 1)

5 A scientist identified 7,452 species of flowers in a rain forest. What is this number rounded to the nearest hundred?

A 7,000   **C** 7,450

B 7,400   **D** 7,500

6 What is the value of the 2 in 23,461,579,000?

F 20 billion   **H** 200 million

G 2 billion   **J** 20 million

7 Which answer lists the students in the order of the rock samples they collected from greatest to least?

ROCK SAMPLES	
Student	*Weight (grams)*
Rocio	2,345
Gregor	1,789
Kira	2,354
Paul	2,298

A Gregor, Paul, Rocio, Kira

B Kira, Rocio, Paul, Gregor

C Gregor, Paul, Rocio, Kira

D Paul, Gregor, Kira, Rocio

8 Look at this number line.

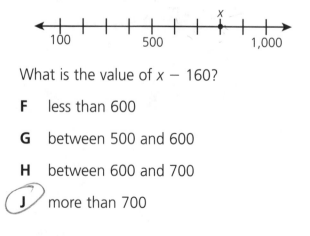

What is the value of x − 160?

F less than 600

G between 500 and 600

H between 600 and 700

J more than 700

9 Arthur told Connie that the rounded price of the car his parents just bought was $9,000. What might the actual price of the car have been?

_____ between $8,500 and $9,499 _____

> To round to the nearest thousand, look at the digit in the hundreds place. To round a number up, this digit must be at least 5: 8,500. To round a number down, this digit must be a 4 or less: 9,499. So the actual price must have been between $8,500 and $9,499.

10 Write four million, five hundred sixty-two thousand in standard form.

_____ 4,562,000 _____

11 Write 46,538 in expanded form.

$(4 \times 10,000) + (6 \times 1,000) + (5 \times 100) + (3 \times 10) + (8 \times 1)$

12 LaToya recorded the total profit from the sale of raffle tickets as $87,146. She totaled the amount on her calculator and realized she had exchanged the hundreds and the ten thousands digits. How much money should LaToya record now?

_____ 17,846 _____

13 The concert at the stadium was attended by 7,553 people. What is this number rounded to the nearest hundred?

_____ 7,600 _____

14 This table shows the inventory list for a T-shirt company. Which color T-shirt are there more of than black but not as many as green?

_____ Red _____

T-SHIRT INVENTORY	
Color	Total
White	12,412
Black	11,927
Blue	12,398
Red	12,089
Green	12,363

15 A certain number is less than one hundred thousand. The digit in the ten thousands place is an odd number greater than 5 and less than 9. The thousands digit is 2 more than the number of the digit in the ten thousands place. The digit in the hundreds place is the number 264 rounded to the hundreds place. The number 57 rounded to the tens place becomes the tens digit. The ones digit equals the number of digits in 86 million in standard form.

Part A

Write the number in standard form.

_____

Part B

Switch the digits in the thousands and tens places. What is the difference between the original number and the switched number? Explain how you got your answer.

_____

_____

_____

_____

_____

_____

_____

Ask yourself—
How many digits are in this number? What is the place value of the digit?

Before you write—
Think about the position of the thousands and tens digits.

Now—
Check your answer. Does it make sense?

1–2 Factors and Multiples

✸ A number is **divisible,** or can be divided evenly, by any number that is a **factor.**

You can tell that a number is divisible by—

- 2 if the ones digit is 0, 2, 4, 6, or 8.

$$3\textbf{6} \qquad 15\textbf{0} \qquad 7,27\textbf{8}$$

- 3 if the sum of the digits is divisible by 3.

$$4,368 \rightarrow 4 + 3 + 6 + 8 = 21 \rightarrow 21 \div 3 = 7$$

- 5 if the ones digit is 5 or 0.

$$1,11\textbf{5} \qquad 3,621,73\textbf{0}$$

- 6 if the number is divisible by 2 and by 3.

$$648 \rightarrow 8 \div 2 = 4$$
$$648 \rightarrow 6 + 4 + 8 = 18 \rightarrow 18 \div 3 = 6$$

- 9 if the sum of the digits is divisible by 9.

$$21,942 \rightarrow 2 + 1 + 9 + 4 + 2 = 18 \rightarrow 18 \div 9 = 2$$

- 10 if the ones digit is 0.

$$38\textbf{0} \qquad 5,71\textbf{0} \qquad 261,93\textbf{0}$$

✸ Any **multiple** of a number is divisible by all of its factors.

Multiples of 6: 6, 12, 18, 24, 30, 36, 42, …

Factors of 6: 1, 2, 3, 6

Every multiple of 6 is divisible by 1, 2, 3, and 6.

$$12 \div \textbf{1} = 12$$
$$18 \div \textbf{2} = 9$$
$$30 \div \textbf{3} = 10$$
$$42 \div \textbf{6} = 7$$

Remember—

Factors are numbers that are multiplied together to get a product.

$$1 \times 8 = 8$$
$$2 \times 4 = 8$$

The factors of 8 are 1, 2, 4, and 8.

Common factors are factors two products share.

Factors of 8: 1, 2, 4, 8
Factors of 12: 1, 2, 3, 4, 6, 12
1, 2, and 4 are common factors of 8 and 12.

The **greatest common factor** (GCF) is the largest factor shared by two numbers.
4 is the GCF of 8 and 12.

Multiples are the products of a number and another factor.
Multiples of 9: 9, 18, 27, 36, 45, …

Common multiples are the multiples that numbers share.
Multiples of 9: 9, 18, 27, 36, 45, …
Multiples of 6: 6, 12, 18, 24, 30, 36, …
18 and 36 are common multiples of 9 and 6.

The **least common multiple** (LCM) is the smallest multiple shared by two numbers.
18 is the LCM of 9 and 6.

1 How many whole numbers between 1 and 100 are divisible by 6 **and** by 10?

A 1   **C** 6

B 3   **D** 9

> Did you choose B? That's right. There are 9 numbers between 1 and 100 divisible by 10; those ending in 0: 10, 20, 30, etc. Of those numbers, only three are multiples of 6: 30, 60, and 90.

2 Which of these is **not** a factor of 40?

F 2   **H** 6

G 5   **J** 8

3 Diahn and Eduardo paid the same price for some candy. Diahn paid with dimes and Eduardo paid with quarters. Neither one received any change. What could be the amount of money they paid?

A $2.50

B $2.75

C $3.10

D $3.25

4 Which set shows all the factors of 36?

F {1, 6, 36}

G {1, 3, 4, 6, 9, 12, 18, 24, 36}

H {1, 2, 3, 4, 6, 9, 12, 18, 24, 36}

J {1, 2, 3, 4, 6, 9, 12, 18, 36}

5 A shop sold socks in packages of 5 pairs. Which number could be the number of pairs of socks in a display?

A 403   **C** 456

B 445   **D** 581

6 What is the least common multiple of 16 and 24?

F 2   **H** 48

G 8   **J** 96

7 A supermarket sells sports drinks in packs that contain 6 bottles each. Which of these could **not** be the number of bottles of sports drinks on the store's shelf?

A 258   **C** 285

B 270   **D** 294

8 How many whole numbers less than 50 are divisible by 3?

F 16   **H** 25

G 17   **J** 50

12

9 What's the least common multiple of 10 and 12?

_____*60*_____

> The least common multiple is the smallest multiple shared by two numbers. So find the multiples of 10: 10, 20, 30, 40, 50, 60, 70, 80, 90, ... Then find the multiples of 12: 12, 24, 36, 48, 60, 72, 84, 96, 108, ... Then look for the smallest number in both sets: 60. The LCM of 10 and 12 is 60.

10 Explain how you can tell if a five-digit number is divisible by 6 without actually dividing it. Then write an example.

_____

_____

11 Audrey has 48 CDs. She wants to store them in stacks of equal size. What is the largest number of CDs she could have in each stack? Show your work.

_____

12 Each row in a parking lot has 15 spaces. How many spaces could be in the parking lot? Give at least 5 possibilities. Explain how you know.

_____

_____

13 A group of 4 students ordered pizza for a party. If a pizza is cut into 6 slices, what is the least number of pizzas that must be ordered so everyone gets the same number of slices? Show your work.

_____

14 Find the greatest common factor (GCF) of 90 and 135. Show your work.

_____

15 Tracy's Cup Company puts 96 cups in each plastic bag for sale. Each bag has more than 2 and fewer than 9 stacks of cups. Each stack contains more than 2 cups.

Part A

How many stacks and cups per stack are possible? Name all the possible combinations of ways the cups might be packed in a bag.

_____

_____

Ask yourself—
What are the factors of 96?

Part B

Explain how you solved the problem.

_____

Before you write—
Think about the steps you used to solve the problem.

_____

_____

_____

_____

_____

_____

_____

_____

Now—
Check your answer. Does it make sense?

1–3 Fractions, Decimals, and Percents

✹ A **fraction, decimal,** and a **percent** can name the same number.

$$\frac{60}{100} = \frac{60}{10} = \frac{3}{5}$$

$$\frac{60}{100} = 0.60 = 0.6$$

$$\frac{60}{100} = 0.60 = 60\%$$

These answers are **equivalent.** They name the same number in different forms.

✹ To change a fraction to a decimal, divide the numerator by the denominator.

$$1\frac{2}{5} = \frac{7}{5} = 5\overline{)7.0} = 1.4$$

✹ To change a decimal to a fraction, put the decimal number over the place value of the digit in the rightmost column.

$$0.4 = \frac{4}{10} \qquad 0.345 = \frac{345}{1,000}$$

Use the greatest common factor (GCF) of the numerator and denominator to find the **lowest terms,** or simplest form.

$$\frac{4}{10} = \frac{4 \div 2}{10 \div 2} = \frac{2}{5} \qquad \frac{345}{1,000} = \frac{345 \div 5}{1,000 \div 5} = \frac{69}{200}$$

✹ To compare fractions with unlike denominators, change the fractions to equivalent fractions by finding the **least common multiple (LCM)** of the denominators.

Is $\frac{2}{3}$ greater than or less than $\frac{3}{4}$?

First find the LCM of 3 and 4:

Multiples of 3: 3, 6, 9, 12, 15, …

Multiples of 4: 4, 8, 12, 16, …

The LCM of 3 and 4 is 12.

Then change the fractions to equivalent fractions:

$$\frac{2 \times 4}{3 \times 4} = \frac{8}{12} \qquad \frac{3 \times 3}{4 \times 3} = \frac{9}{12}$$

The fraction $\frac{8}{12}$ is less than $\frac{9}{12}$ so $\frac{2}{3} < \frac{3}{4}$.

Remember—

A fraction can name part of a whole.

Jack ate $\frac{1}{2}$ of the pie.

A fraction can name part of a group or set. There were 5 girls in a class of 12 students. So $\frac{5}{12}$ of the students were girls.

The **terms** of a fraction are the numerator and denominator.

$\frac{9}{15}$ ← **numerator**
← **denominator**

To compare decimals, compare the digits in the same places. Compare tenths to tenths, hundredths to hundredths, and so on.

0.60 > 0.467
6 tenths > 4 tenths

Decimals are rounded to a place value the same way as whole numbers. Look at the digit in the next place to the right. If the digit is 4 or less, round down. If it is 5 or more, round up.

0.138 rounded to the nearest hundredth is 0.14

To change a decimal to a percent, move the decimal point two places to the **right** and write a percent sign.

0.76 = 76%

Read each problem. Circle the letter of the best answer.

1 Only $\frac{2}{5}$ of Lake Minnehaha is free of weeds. What is this fraction expressed as a decimal?

A 0.2   **C** 0.4

B 0.25   **D** 0.45

> Did you select C? That's correct. To change a fraction to a decimal, divide the numerator by the denominator:
>
> $$\frac{2}{5} = 2 \div 5 = 5\overline{)2.0} = 0.4$$

2 During a rainstorm, sixty-eight hundredths of an inch of rain fell. What is this number written as a decimal?

F 0.068   **H** 6.8

G 0.68   **J** 68.00

3 What is the value of *z* on this number line?

A 2.2   **C** 2.4

B 2.3   **D** 3.15

4 Arnie and Chamiqua have decorated $\frac{3}{8}$ of the cupcakes. What fraction of the batch still needs to be decorated?

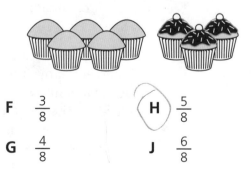

F $\frac{3}{8}$ **H** $\frac{5}{8}$

G $\frac{4}{8}$ **J** $\frac{6}{8}$

5 At the supermarket, Bart bought 1.37 pounds of chicken. Which of these is the same as 1.37?

A $1\frac{1}{37}$ **C** $1\frac{3}{100}$

B $1\frac{37}{10}$ **D** $1\frac{37}{100}$

6 A grizzly bear can eat about $\frac{1}{6}$ of its weight in a single meal. If a certain grizzly eats 60 pounds of salmon, about how much does that grizzly weigh?

F 10 pounds   **H** 360 pounds

G 180 pounds   **J** 600 pounds

7 Lisa won a swimming race with a time of 28.75 seconds. The school newspaper reported her time to the nearest tenth of a second. What time did it report?

A 29 seconds

B 28.8 seconds

C 28.75 seconds

D 28.7 seconds

8 What is $\frac{9}{36}$ expressed as a percent?

F 4%   **H** 32%

G 25%   **J** 40%

9 What temperature does this thermometer show?

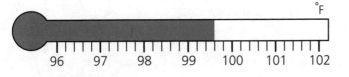

_99.6°_

> Each tick mark on the thermometer is 0.2°. The temperature falls
> between 99° and 100°. Count by 0.2° from 99° to reach 99.6°.

10 What is $\frac{9}{24}$ in lowest terms? Show your work.

_____

11 A science class potted 125 bean plants for an experiment. This
number was 20% of the total plants needed for the experiment.
How many plants are needed in all? Show your work.

_____

12 Mark and label 1.4 on the number line.

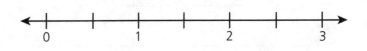

13 A solar-powered airplane reaches a top speed of 84.72 km per
hour. Express this as a mixed number in lowest terms. Show
your work.

_____

14 The table below shows the final results in a 100-yard sprint.
Chuck won the race. Arrange the rest of the times in order
from fastest to slowest.

_____

100-YARD SPRINT	
Racer	_Time (seconds)_
Anwar	12.814
Sandra	12.416
Ernie	12.841
Irene	12.184
Chuck	11.998

15 Five students have a book report due next week. The following shows the portions of the book each student has read this week:

$$\frac{3}{8}, \ \frac{8}{16}, \ \frac{56}{64}, \ \frac{5}{20}, \ \frac{24}{32}$$

Part A

Change each fraction to a decimal. Then label each decimal on the number line with the equivalent fraction. Show your work.

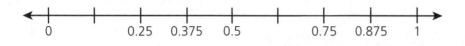

_____

Part B

Explain how you changed the fractions to decimals and how you knew where to place them on the number line.

_____

_____

_____

_____

_____

_____

_____

1–4 Ratios and Proportions

✹ A **ratio** is a comparison of two numbers.

> A basket of fruit had 5 apples and 7 pears. The ratio of apples to pears is 5 to 7.

Ratios are often written with a colon (:) or as a fraction.

apples to pears	5:7 or $\frac{5}{7}$	pears to fruit	7:12 or $\frac{7}{12}$
pears to apples	7:5 or $\frac{7}{5}$	fruit to apples	12:5 or $\frac{12}{5}$
apples to fruit	5:12 or $\frac{5}{12}$	fruit to pears	12:7 or $\frac{12}{7}$

✹ A **proportion** is a statement that says two ratios are equal.

$$\frac{5}{7} = \frac{15}{21}$$

> This proportion says that the ratio 5 to 7 is equal to the ratio 15 to 21.

To check if the two ratios are equal, find the **cross products.** Multiply the means and the extremes. If the products are equal, the proportion is true.

$$\frac{5}{7} \overset{?}{=} \frac{15}{21}$$
$$5 \times 21 = 7 \times 15$$
$$105 = 105$$

✹ You can use cross products to find the missing term in a proportion.

> Julia ate 3 slices of apple with 2 ounces of dipping sauce. Her sister ate 9 slices and used sauce at the same rate. How much sauce did Julia's sister use?

> Let s stand for the amount of sauce Julia's sister used. Set up a proportion. Be sure the terms are in the same order in each ratio. Then solve for s.

$$\frac{3}{2} = \frac{9}{s}$$
$$3 \times s = 2 \times 9$$
$$3s = 18$$
$$s = \frac{18}{3}$$
$$s = 6$$

> Julia's sister used 6 ounces of dipping sauce.

Finish Line Math–Level F

19

Remember—

Read each problem carefully. The order of the terms of a ratio is important.

$\frac{5}{7}$ is **not** the same as the ratio $\frac{7}{5}$.

A **rate** is a comparison using different units.

$$\frac{45 \text{ miles}}{1 \text{ hour}}$$

means   extremes

The means and extremes are easier to see when the proportion is written using colons.

extremes
↓   ↓
5:7 = 15:21
↑   ↑
means

Be sure the missing term is a proportion is in the correct place.

$$\frac{\text{apples}}{\text{sauce}} = \frac{3}{2} = \frac{9}{s}$$

1 Elena's hanging plant grew 6 inches in 4 months. At that rate, how many inches will it grow in 10 months?

 A   10 inches   **C**   16 inches

 B   15 inches   **D**   24 inches

> Did you pick B? That's right. Since the plant is expected to grow at the same rate, set up a proportion where n represents the missing inches. Solve for n by cross multiplying:
> $$\frac{4}{6} = \frac{10}{n}$$
> $$4 \times n = 6 \times 10$$
> $$4n = 60$$
> $$\frac{4n}{4} = \frac{60}{4}$$
> $$n = 15 \text{ inches}$$

2 Walter's Fuel truck could deliver 20 gallons of oil per minute into a home oil tank. At that rate, how long would it take to pump 250 gallons into a tank?

 F   5 minutes   **H**   12.5 minutes

 G   10 minutes   **J**   20 minutes

3 If 2 pounds of hamburger feeds 3 people, which number sentence could be used to find the number of pounds of hamburger needed to feed 15 people?

 A $\frac{\square}{3} = \frac{2}{15}$ **C** $\frac{\square}{15} = \frac{3}{2}$

 B $\frac{\square}{3} = \frac{15}{2}$ **D** $\frac{\square}{15} = \frac{2}{3}$

4 It took 2 minutes to fill a bathtub with water to a depth of 4 inches. At that rate, how long would it take to fill the tub to 12 inches?

 F   5 minutes   **H**   8 minutes

 G   6 minutes   **J**   18 minutes

5 A flower arrangement had 20 carnations and 13 roses. Which of the following shows the ratio of carnations to all flowers in the arrangement?

 A $\frac{13}{20}$ **C** $\frac{20}{33}$

 B $\frac{20}{13}$ **D** $\frac{33}{20}$

6 A class sold 8 pizzas for a total of $48. Each pizza cost the same amount. At that rate, how much money would the class make by selling 15 pizzas?

 F $63   **H** $90

 G $71   **J** $120

7 If 7 quarts of water are needed to boil 2 pounds of spaghetti noodles, which number sentence could be solved to find the number of quarts of water needed to boil 8 pounds of spaghetti noodles?

 A $\frac{2}{8} = \frac{\square}{7}$ **C** $\frac{7}{8} = \frac{\square}{2}$

 B $\frac{7}{2} = \frac{\square}{8}$ **D** $\frac{2}{7} = \frac{\square}{8}$

8 Jeremy has missed 6 days of school this year. Magda has missed 4 days. Which of the following represents the ratio of Magda's missed days to Jeremy's?

 F $\frac{6}{4}$ **H** $\frac{3}{2}$

 G $\frac{4}{10}$ **J** $\frac{2}{3}$

20

9 Nicole's heart beats 135 times in 2 minutes. Assuming that it continues to beat at the same rate, write a proportion that could be solved to find the number of times Nicole's heart beats, b, in 60 minutes.

$$\frac{135}{2} = \frac{b}{60}$$

> Set up a proportion to solve for the missing number of beats in 60 minutes:
> 135 beats in 2 minutes equals b beats in 60 minutes:
> $\frac{135}{2} = \frac{b}{60}$. Both ratios are $\frac{\text{beats}}{\text{time}}$.

10 There are 34 students are in Mr. Brown's class. Twelve students are wearing shorts. Write the ratio in lowest terms of students in Mr. Brown's class that are **not** wearing shorts compared to the whole class.

_____

11 At a party, 4 out of 5 guests had chocolate cake. The party had 45 guests. Write a proportion that you could solve to find the number of guests, n, that had chocolate cake.

_____

12 Solve this proportion to find the missing term. Show your work.

$$\frac{5}{16} = \frac{55}{m}$$

_____

13 An airplane flies 1,200 miles in 3 hours. Write and solve a proportion to find how many miles, m, it will fly in 7 hours. Show your work.

_____

14 This table shows the results of a 12-minute hot dog eating contest.

HOT DOG EATING CONTEST	
Contestant	*Number of Hot Dogs*
Jorge	12
Lou	20
Frankie	15
Cassie	10
Pat	18

Part A

Express in simplest form the ratio of hot dogs Frankie ate to the hot dogs eaten by all the contestants in the contest.

_____

Part B

If Cassie continues eating hot dogs at the same rate, how many minutes will it take her to eat the same number as the winner of the contest? Write and solve a proportion. Explain how you found your answer.

_____

_____

_____

_____

_____

_____

Ask yourself—
How many hot dogs did Frankie eat? How many hot dogs were eaten by all the contestants?

Before you write—
Think about the units described in the problem. Be sure the order of the terms is the same on both sides of the equal sign.

Now—
Check your answer. Does it make sense?

1–R Number and Number Relations Review

Read each problem. Circle the letter of the best answer.

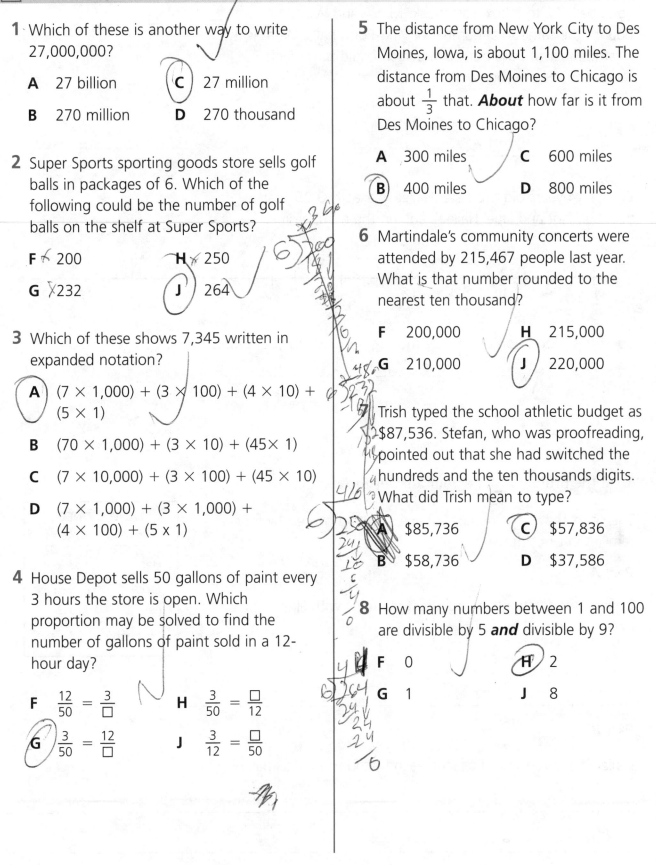

1 Which of these is another way to write 27,000,000?

A 27 billion

C 27 million

B 270 million

D 270 thousand

2 Super Sports sporting goods store sells golf balls in packages of 6. Which of the following could be the number of golf balls on the shelf at Super Sports?

F 200

H 250

G 232

J 264

3 Which of these shows 7,345 written in expanded notation?

A $(7 \times 1,000) + (3 \times 100) + (4 \times 10) + (5 \times 1)$

B $(70 \times 1,000) + (3 \times 10) + (45 \times 1)$

C $(7 \times 10,000) + (3 \times 100) + (45 \times 10)$

D $(7 \times 1,000) + (3 \times 1,000) + (4 \times 100) + (5 \times 1)$

4 House Depot sells 50 gallons of paint every 3 hours the store is open. Which proportion may be solved to find the number of gallons of paint sold in a 12-hour day?

F $\frac{12}{50} = \frac{3}{\square}$

H $\frac{3}{50} = \frac{\square}{12}$

G $\frac{3}{50} = \frac{12}{\square}$

J $\frac{3}{12} = \frac{\square}{50}$

5 The distance from New York City to Des Moines, Iowa, is about 1,100 miles. The distance from Des Moines to Chicago is about $\frac{1}{3}$ that. **About** how far is it from Des Moines to Chicago?

A 300 miles

C 600 miles

B 400 miles

D 800 miles

6 Martindale's community concerts were attended by 215,467 people last year. What is that number rounded to the nearest ten thousand?

F 200,000

H 215,000

G 210,000

J 220,000

7 Trish typed the school athletic budget as $87,536. Stefan, who was proofreading, pointed out that she had switched the hundreds and the ten thousands digits. What did Trish mean to type?

A $85,736

C $57,836

B $58,736

D $37,586

8 How many numbers between 1 and 100 are divisible by 5 **and** divisible by 9?

F 0

H 2

G 1

J 8

9 Marcy buys Ping-Pong balls in cartons of 9. Winton buys Ping-Pong balls 12 to a box. Last week, Marcy and Winton both bought the same total number of Ping-Pong balls. What is the least number of balls that each person could have been purchased? Show your work.

_____

10 Evan is 14 years old. His sister Hailee is exactly 3.25 years younger. Plot and label Hailee's age on the number line.

11 Solve this proportion to find the missing term. Show your work.

$$\frac{12}{25} = \frac{n}{125}$$

_____

12 The chart shows the number of acres of land owned by four families in Lincolntown.

LAND OWNED	
Family	*Acres*
Hafz	$3\frac{1}{2}$
Jackson	$3\frac{1}{4}$
Levy	$2\frac{5}{8}$
Mutumbo	$4\frac{7}{10}$

Part A

Change the fractions to equivalent fractions with like denominators. Show your work.

_____

Part B

Explain how you would change each fraction to a decimal.

_____

_____

24

2–1 Operation Sense

✹ When **multiplying** fractions or decimals greater than 1, the product is always *larger* than the factors, unless one factor is 1.

Shiori walks 2.25 miles 3 days a week. How many miles does she walk in a week?

$$3 \times 2.25 = 6.75 \text{ miles}$$

✹ When **multiplying** fractions or decimals less than 1, the product is always *less* than the larger factor.

A pencil weighs 0.25 gram. How much would 5 pencils weigh?

$$5 \times 0.25 = 1.25 \text{ grams}$$

One book weighs $\frac{1}{2}$ pound. How much would 3 copies of the book weigh?

$$3 \times \frac{1}{2} = \frac{3}{2} = 1\frac{1}{2} \text{ pounds}$$

✹ When **dividing** fractions or decimals greater than 1, the quotient is always *smaller* than the dividend, unless you are dividing by 1.

Mother used 3.5 pounds of cherries to make 2 pies of equal size. If they were divided equally, how many cherries did each pie get?

$$3.5 \div 2 = 1.75 \text{ pounds}$$

A $4\frac{1}{2}$-pound bag of nuts has to be put into $1\frac{1}{2}$-pound bags. How many bags will be used?

$$4\frac{1}{2} \div 1\frac{1}{2} = \frac{9}{2} \div \frac{3}{2} = \frac{9}{2} \times \frac{2}{3} = \frac{18}{6} = 3 \text{ bags}$$

✹ When **dividing** fractions or decimals less than 1, the quotient is always *larger* than the dividend.

A recipe calls for $2\frac{1}{4}$ cups of flour. How many $\frac{1}{4}$-cup scoops of flour is that?

$$2\frac{1}{4} \div \frac{1}{4} = \frac{9}{4} \div \frac{1}{4} = \frac{9}{4} \times \frac{4}{1} = \frac{36}{4} = 9 \text{ scoops}$$

Remember—

Add to combine groups.

Ramón has $\frac{3}{4}$ of a pie. Jessie has $\frac{1}{4}$ of a pie. How much pie do they have together?

addends
↓   ↓
$$\frac{3}{4} + \frac{1}{4} = 1$$
↑
sum

Subtract to find how many are left or to compare numbers.

Joey has 1.5 bags of pennies. Ivana has 0.5 bag of pennies. How many more bags of pennies does Joey have than Ivana?

$$\begin{array}{r} 1.5 \\ -\ 0.5 \\ \hline 1.0 \end{array}$$ ← minuend
← subtrahend
← difference

Multiply to combine groups of equal size.

How many ducks are in 5 flocks of 40 each?

factors
↓   ↓
$$5 \times 40 = 200$$
↑
product

Divide to break groups into equal-sized sets.

A carton holds 12 eggs. How many cartons are needed for 288 eggs?

dividend
↓
$$288 \div 12 = 24 \text{ ← quotient}$$
↑
divisor

Read each problem. Circle the letter of the best answer.

1 Victor uses a $\frac{1}{2}$-cup scoop to measure $3\frac{1}{2}$ cups of peanuts. Which number sentence could he solve to find the number of $\frac{1}{2}$-cup scoops he needs?

A $3\frac{1}{2} + \frac{1}{2} = \square$ **C** $3\frac{1}{2} \times \frac{1}{2} = \square$

B $3\frac{1}{2} - \frac{1}{2} = \square$ **D** $3\frac{1}{2} \div \frac{1}{2} = \square$

> Did you choose D? That's right. To find how many $\frac{1}{2}$-cup scoops are in $3\frac{1}{2}$ cups, divide $3\frac{1}{2}$ into equal-sized parts of $\frac{1}{2}$ cup: $3\frac{1}{2} \div \frac{1}{2} = \square$.

2 Which of these has the least value?

F $1,000 + 20$ **H** $1,000 \div 20$

G $1,000 - 20$ **J** $1,000 \times 20$

3 A group of 23 students went on a field trip to a museum. Each student brought $4.50 for lunch and $2.25 for admission. Which number sentence gives the total cost of the field trip for the 23 students?

A $(\$4.50 \times \$2.25) \div 23 = \square$

B $(\$4.50 + \$2.25) \div 23 = \square$

C $23 \times (\$4.50 \times \$2.25) = \square$

D $23 \times (\$4.50 + \$2.25) = \square$

4 Last year, Quick Mart sold 500 gallons of gas per day at $0.85 a gallon. This year, the price of gas has doubled. How many gallons must be sold per day to total the same amount of money as last year?

F 250 gallons   **H** 750 gallons

G 500 gallons   **J** 1,000 gallons

5 Yvonne has $400 to spend on refreshments for 5 school dances. Which of these expressions would help her to find the amount she can spend for each dance?

A 400×5 **C** $400 - 5$

B $400 \div 5$ **D** $400 + 5$

6 Look at this number sentence.

$$30 \div \square = 25$$

Which describes the number that goes in the box to make the number sentence true?

F a number greater than 2

G a number between 1 and 2

H a number between $\frac{1}{2}$ and 1

J a number less than $\frac{1}{2}$

7 Tomas used $5\frac{1}{3}$ pounds of nails on a project. Of that amount, $\frac{2}{3}$ were finishing nails. Which number sentence could Tomas solve to find the amount of finishing nails?

A $5\frac{1}{3} + \frac{2}{3} = \square$ **C** $5\frac{1}{3} \times \frac{2}{3} = \square$

B $5\frac{1}{3} - \frac{2}{3} = \square$ **D** $5\frac{1}{3} \div \frac{2}{3} = \square$

8 Which describes the number that goes in the box to make this number sentence true?

$$50 \times \square = 40$$

F a number less than $\frac{1}{2}$

G a number between $\frac{1}{2}$ and 1

H a number between 1 and $1\frac{1}{2}$

J a number greater than $1\frac{1}{2}$

9 Which of these expressions will have the larger quotient?

$$0.7 \div 0.35 \qquad 0.7 \div 0.035$$

_____ *0.7 ÷ 0.035* _____

> When dividing by a decimal less than 1, the quotient is always larger than the dividend. The smaller the divisor, the larger the quotient: $0.7 \div 0.35 = 2$ and $0.7 \div 0.035 = 20$. The expression $0.7 \div 0.035$ has the larger quotient.

10 Mrs. Mustafa has $3.60 in her pocket. She wants to use it all to buy as many 45¢ packs of gum as she can. Write a number sentence to find how many packs of gum she can buy. Use ☐ for the result.

_____

11 A builder bought 4 building lots of $\frac{3}{4}$ acre each and 7 lots of $1\frac{2}{3}$ acres each. Explain how you could find the total amount of acres the builder bought.

_____

_____

12 Water comes out of a hose at a rate of $\frac{3}{4}$ gallon per minute. A hose is run for $2\frac{1}{2}$ hours into a swimming pool. Write a number sentence that could be used to find how much water went into the pool in $2\frac{1}{2}$ hours. Use ☐ for the result.

_____

13 Three friends picked strawberries at a farm. Dorothy picked 10 pints, Cheryl picked 8 pints, and Sid picked 15 pints. The friends want to share the strawberries equally. Write a number sentence that you could solve to find how many pints each friend should get. Use ☐ for the result.

_____

28

▣ Read the problem. Write your answer for each part.

14 Last year, Cahill's Farm sold 2,800 bushels of corn at $13.50 per bushel. This year, corn prices have dropped to $6.75 per bushel.

Part A

Will the number of bushels of corn need to increase or decrease to equal last year's income?

_____

Part B

Explain how you found your answer.

_____

_____

_____

_____

_____

_____

_____

_____

Ask yourself—
Did the price of a bushel of corn increase or decrease? Will the farm have to sell more or less corn to make up the difference?

Before you write—
Think about the operations you could use to find how many bushels they need to sell this year to equal last year's sales.

Now—
Check your answer. Does it make sense?

2–2 Properties and Order of Operations

❋ **Inverse operations** are opposite operations that can be used to undo each other.

Addition and subtraction are inverse operations. You can add to check subtraction or subtract to check addition.

$$3\tfrac{1}{2} - \tfrac{1}{2} = 3 \text{ because } 3 + \tfrac{1}{2} = 3\tfrac{1}{2}$$

Multiplication and division are inverse operations. You can multiply to check division or divide to check multiplication.

$$5.25 \div 0.5 = 10.5 \text{ because } 10.5 \times 0.5 = 5.25$$

❋ When an expression has more than one operation, complete the operations in a certain order.

First, complete any operations within parentheses.

$$9 + 3 \times (5 - 2) - 6 \div 3$$
$$9 + 3 \times 3 - 6 \div 3$$

Next, multiply or divide in order from left to right.

$$9 + 3 \times 3 - 6 \div 3$$
$$9 + 9 - 6 \div 3$$
$$9 + 9 - 2$$

Finally, add or subtract in order from left to right.

$$9 + 9 - 2$$
$$18 - 2$$
$$16$$

Remember—

The **commutative property** says that numbers may be added or multiplied in any order.

$$1.8 \times 0.6 = 0.6 \times 1.8$$

The commutative property is **not** true for subtraction or division.

The **associative property** says numbers can be grouped in any order to add or multiply.

$$(\tfrac{1}{3} + \tfrac{1}{4}) + 6 = \tfrac{1}{3} + (\tfrac{1}{4} + 6)$$

Parentheses ( ) are grouping symbols. Always work within parentheses first.

The associative property is **not** true for subtraction or division.

The **identity element** of addition is 0. If you add 0 to any number, the sum is that number.

$$24 + 0 = 24$$
$$8\tfrac{5}{8} + 0 = 8\tfrac{5}{8}$$

The **identity element** for multiplication is 1. If you multiply any number by 1, the product is the number.

$$1 \times \tfrac{1}{4} = \tfrac{1}{1} \times \tfrac{1}{4} = \tfrac{1}{4}$$
$$1 \times 9.216 = 9.216$$

Read each problem. Circle the letter of the best answer.

1 What is the value of this expression?

$$5 + 3 \times (7 - 1)$$

A 23   C 48

B 25   D 64

> Did you choose A? That's correct. First do the operation inside parentheses:
> $5 + 3 \times (7 - 1) = 5 + 3 \times 6$.
> Then multiply: $5 + 3 \times 6 = 5 + 18$.
> Finally, add: $5 + 18 = 23$.

2 Which number sentence shows the commutative property for multiplication?

F $3 \times (4 \times 5) = (3 \times 4) \times 5$

G $3 \times (4 + 5) = (3 \times 4) + (3 \times 5)$

H $(4 \times 5) = (5 \times 4)$

J $(4 + 5) = (5 + 4)$

3 Which of these is **not** true?

A $8 \times 1 = 8$ C $8 \div 0 = 8$

B $8 + 0 = 8$ D $1 \times 8 = 8$

4 Which expression equals 72?

F $36 \div 4 - 3 \times 2$

G $(36 \div 4 - 3) \times 2$

H $36 \div (4 - 3 \times 2)$

J $36 \div (4 - 3) \times 2$

5 If $z \div y = 4$, then which of these must be true?

A $4 + y = z$ C $z \times 4 = y$

B $y \times 4 = z$ D $z - 4 = y$

6 Rosario started with a certain number, added 8, then multiplied by 9. Which sequence of operations could she perform next to return to her starting number?

F divide by 9, then subtract 8

G divide by 9, then add 8

H subtract 8, then divide by 9

J add 8, then divide by 9

7 Which of these expressions has the greatest value?

A $6 + 13 \times 2 + 14$

B $(6 + 13) \times 2 + 14$

C $6 + 13 \times (2 + 14)$

D $(6 + 13) \times (2 + 14)$

8 Which expression makes this number sentence true?

$$(2 \times 15) \times 60 = \square$$

F $(2 + 15) + 60$

G $2 + (15 + 60)$

H $2 \times (15 \times 60)$

J $(2 \times 60) + (15 \times 60)$

30

9 If $a \div b = c$, then $c \times b = a$. Why is this statement true?

<u>   Multiplication and division are inverse operations.   </u>

> Substitute whole numbers for the letters: $a = 6$, $b = 3$, $c = 3$. If $6 \div 3 = 2$, then its inverse is true: $2 \times 3 = 6$. Using this as a model, you can see that multiplication and division are inverse operations.

10 Eva has 12 short-sleeve blouses. If Yolanda buys 1 more blouse she will have 1 times as many as Eva. How many blouses does Yolanda have now?

_____

11 Find the value of $27 - (3 \times 5) \div 5$. Show your work.

_____

12 Tamiqua loaned $15 to Walt on Tuesday. The next day, Walt repaid Tamiqua $15. If Tamiqua started with $35, write a number sentence that she could use to record her business with Walt. Use □ for the result.

_____

13 The Springfield Symphony had 1,893 people at Friday's concert and 3,251 at Saturday's concert. Barry added $1,893 + 3,251$ to get the total attendance for the two days. Anna added $3,251 + 1,893$. Whose sum was greater? Explain how you know.

_____

_____

14 Which expression has the lesser value? Show your work.

$$25 \times (5 - 3) \quad or \quad 25 \times 5 - 3$$

_____

15 In the number sentences below, the same shape always stands for the same number.

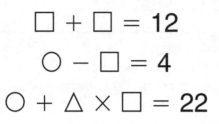

$$\square + \square = 12$$
$$\bigcirc - \square = 4$$
$$\bigcirc + \triangle \times \square = 22$$

Part A

Find the number each shape stands for.

$\square =$ _____ $\bigcirc =$ _____ $\triangle =$ _____

Part B

Explain the steps you took to find your answers.

_____

_____

_____

_____

_____

_____

_____

Ask yourself—
What number added to itself is 12?

Before you write—
Think about the inverse operations you can use to find your answers.

Now—
Check your answer. Does it make sense?

2–R Operation Concepts Review

Read each problem. Circle the letter of the best answer.

1 Which of these expressions has the least value?

  A 2,000 + 2.5   **C** 2,000 × 2.5

  B 2,000 − 2.5   **D** 2,000 ÷ 2.5

2 Brenda started with a certain number and subtracted 8. Then she divided the result by 3. Which sequence of operations could she perform to return to her starting number?

  F add 8, then multiply by 3

  G subtract 8, then multiply by 3

  H multiply by 3, then add 8

  J multiply by 8, then add 3

3 Amelia brought 10 marshmallows on a camping trip. Darcy and Tony brought 24 together and Frank brought 18. Which number sentence could they use to find how many marshmallows each one should get if they shared them equally?

  A □ = 10 + 24 + 18 ÷ 4

  B □ = (10 + 24 + 18) ÷ 4

  C □ = 4 ÷ 10 + 24 + 18

  D □ = 4 ÷ (10 + 24 + 18)

4 What is the value of this expression?

$$7 + 8 \times (9 - 2)$$

  F 63   **H** 105

  G 77   **J** 392

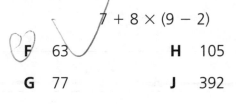

5 Which of these describes the number that goes in the box to make this number sentence true?

$$56 \times \square = 63$$

  A a number greater than 2

  B a number between 1 and 2

  C a number between $\frac{1}{2}$ and 1

  D a number less than $\frac{1}{2}$

6 Which of the following expressions has the greatest value?

  F (5 + 6) + 7   **H** 5 × (6 + 7)

  G 5 + (6 + 7)   **J** (5 + 6) × 7

7 Hernando needs to put $8\frac{1}{2}$ pints of oil into the engine of his car. He only has $\frac{1}{2}$-pint containers of oil. Which number sentence could he solve to find the number of $\frac{1}{2}$-pint containers he will need?

  A $8\frac{1}{2} + \frac{1}{2} = \square$

  B $8\frac{1}{2} - \frac{1}{2} = \square$

  C $8\frac{1}{2} \div \frac{1}{2} = \square$

  D $8\frac{1}{2} \times \frac{1}{2} = \square$

8 If $r - s = 3$, which of these must be true?

  F $s - r = 3$ **H** $s + 3 = r$

  G $r + 3 = s$ **J** $3 - s = r$

9 Last year, Sea Air sold 6,000 tickets to Puerto Rico at a certain price. This year, a ticket to Puerto Rico costs half as much as last year. How many tickets will Sea Air have to sell this year to equal last year's income from that route? Explain your answer.

_____

_____

10 What is the value of the following expression? Show your work.

$$(15 - 12) \times 5$$

_____

11 Hassan did 5 laps around the 400-meter track. Jed ran 4 laps around the same track. Write a number sentence to find how many meters they ran together. Use □ for the result.

_____

Read the problem. Write your answer for each part.

12 Janet wrote this equation for Felix.

$$\square \times \triangle = \bigcirc$$

Each shape represents a number **not** equal to zero.

Part A

Write another equation that must be true if Janet's equation is true.

_____

Part B

Explain why the equation you wrote must be true. Use real numbers as examples.

_____

_____

3–1 Operations with Whole Numbers and Decimals

✸ To **multiply a whole number and a decimal,** multiply the same way as whole numbers. Then count the number of decimal places in the decimal factor. Place the decimal point in the product that many places from the right.

$$\begin{array}{r} 27.8 \\ \times\ 12 \\ \hline 556 \\ 2780 \\ \hline 333.6 \end{array}$$

The factor has 1 decimal place. So count 1 place from the right in the product and place the point there.

✸ Dividing a whole number by a whole number sometimes results in a **decimal quotient.** Divide the numbers and add a decimal point to the dividend and the quotient when there is a whole number remainder. Add a zero to the dividend, bring it down to the remainder and then continue dividing. Add more zeros if necessary.

$$\begin{array}{r} 4.25 \\ 8\,)\overline{34.00} \\ \underline{32} \\ 20 \\ \underline{16} \\ 40 \\ \underline{40} \end{array}$$

There is a remainder of 2. Add a decimal point to the dividend and the quotient. Add a zero to the dividend, bring it down to the remainder, and continue dividing.

✸ To **estimate** products and quotients with decimals, round to the nearest whole number. Then multiply or divide the rounded numbers.

Angela paid $5.75 for tolls in 3 weeks. About how much did she spend in the 3 weeks?

Round the amount to a whole number:

$5.75 rounds to $6.00

Then multiply the rounded number:

$3 \times \$6.00 = \$18.00$

Angela spent about $18.00 in tolls.

Remember—

Add and subtract decimal numbers the same way you add and subtract whole numbers. Be sure to line up the decimal points first.

$$\begin{array}{r} 8.13 \\ -0.2 \\ \hline 7.93 \end{array}$$

To round a number to a certain place, look at the digit in the next place to the right. If it is 5, 6, 7, 8, or 9, round up.

58 rounds up to 60

If it is 4, 3, 2, or 1, round down.

33 rounds down to 30

Read each problem. Circle the letter of the best answer.

1 A team of 4 is running a 26-mile race. Each team member will run the same distance. How far will each member run?

A 104 miles   **C** 6.5 miles

B 65 miles   **D** 2.6 miles

Did you choose C? That's right. You can solve the problem by dividing the number of miles by the number of team members:

$$\begin{array}{r} 6.5 \\ 4\overline{)26.0} \\ \underline{24} \\ 2\;0 \\ \underline{2\;0} \end{array}$$

2 The school budget included $20,000 for art supplies. The school actually spent $17,248 of these funds. How much of the $20,000 was **not** spent?

F $2,752   **H** $3,752

G $2,762   **J** $3,762

3 Jamal finds that a snail moves at a rate of 1.84 centimeters every 1 hour. If it continues to move at the same rate, how far will it go in 10 hours?

A 0.184 cm   **C** 18.4 cm

B 11.84 cm   **D** 184 cm

4 The skating club put on 4 performances last week. The total attendance was 27,638. If the attendance each night was about the same, what is the best estimate of the attendance for each performance?

F 6,000   **H** 70,000

G 7,000   **J** 80,000

5 Felicity walked 6.07 miles on Friday, 5.21 miles on Saturday, and 4.18 miles on Sunday. **About** how many total miles did she walk?

A between 13 and 14 miles

B between 14 and 15 miles

C between 15 and 16 miles

D between 16 and 17 miles

6 Jason earns $6.45 per hour working at the deli. If he works 16 hours in one week, how much money will he earn?

F $22.45   **H** $51.60

G $38.70   **J** $103.20

7 Doughnuts sell for $4.79 a dozen at Betty's Breakfasts. **About** how much would Joel expect to pay for 3 dozen doughnuts?

A $8.00   **C** $12.00

B $10.00   **D** $15.00

8 The Cortez family bought 2 adult tickets and 3 children's tickets to a movie. How much did they spend all together?

NOW SHOWING
BASES LOADED

ADULTS	CHILDREN
$8.50	$5.50

F $23.50   **H** $33.50

G $27.50   **J** $47.50

□ **Read each problem. Write your answer.**

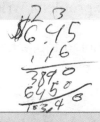

9 What is the best estimate of 785 ÷ 4?

_____ about 200 _____

> Round the dividend to the nearest hundred. To decide whether to round up or down, look at the digit to the right of the place you're rounding to. The digit is 8. The digit is larger than 5, so round up to the next hundreds digit: 785 rounds to 800. Then divide: 800 ÷ 4 = 200.

10 A class sold coupon books to help pay for a trip to a Broadway show. Mrs. Benitez's class sold 178 books, Mr. Clark's class sold 223 books, and Ms. Arnold's class sold 229. How many books did the three classes sell all together? Show your work.

_____

11 What is the best estimate of 29.7 × 7.8?

_____

12 On July 5, a cornstalk was 0.69 meter tall. By August 4, it was 2.1 meters tall. By how much did the cornstalk's height increase? Show your work.

_____

13 A canoe trip will cost a total of $485. If 25 people share the cost equally, **about** how much will each one pay?

_____

14 Mark bought 3 shirts at $12.75 each and 2 pairs of shorts at $21.50 each at an end-of-summer sale. How much did he spend in total? Show your work.

_____

15 For a camping trip, a party of 5 purchased 2 tents, 3 lanterns, and 5 sleeping bags.

$12.99 $45.99 $69.96

Part A

What is the total that they spent on the camping equipment? Show your work.

_____

Part B

If the campers split the cost of the equipment equally, **about** how much will each have to pay? Explain how you found your answer.

_____

_____

_____

_____

_____

Ask yourself—
What operations can I use to find the total when I combine groups of equal size? Of different sizes?

Before you write—
Think about how to round to the nearest whole number.

Now—
Check your answer. Does it make sense?

3–2 Operations with Fractions

✴ To add or subtract **fractions with like denominators,** simply add or subtract the numerators, the denominators stay the same.

$$\frac{2}{4} + \frac{1}{4} = \frac{3}{4} \qquad \frac{5}{8} - \frac{3}{8} = \frac{2}{8} = \frac{1}{4}$$

✴ To add or subtract **fractions with unlike denominators,** first rewrite them as equivalent fractions with like denominators. Start by finding the least common denominator (LCD) of the two numbers.

$$\frac{3}{4} - \frac{2}{3} = \square$$

The least common denominator is the same as the least common multiple (LCM) of the denominators.

Multiples of 4: 4, 8, 12, 16, …

Multiples of 3: 3, 6, 9, 12, …

The least common multiple of 4 and 3 is 12, so the least common denominator is 12.

Then rewrite the fractions as equivalent fractions with the least common denominator.

Multiply $\frac{3}{4}$ by $\frac{3}{3}$ for higher terms:

$$\frac{3}{4} \times \frac{3}{3} = \frac{9}{12}$$

Multiply $\frac{2}{3}$ by $\frac{4}{4}$ for higher terms:

$$\frac{2}{3} \times \frac{4}{4} = \frac{8}{12}$$

Then subtract the fractions:

$$\frac{9}{12} - \frac{8}{12} = \frac{1}{12}$$

✴ To multiply a whole number and a fraction, change the whole number to a fraction by putting a 1 in the denominator. Then multiply the numerators together and the denominators together.

$$\frac{3}{5} \times 3 = \frac{3}{5} \times \frac{3}{1} = \frac{9}{5} = 1\frac{4}{5}$$

Remember—

$$\frac{4}{9} \begin{array}{l} \leftarrow \textbf{numerator} \\ \leftarrow \textbf{denominator} \end{array}$$

To reduce a fraction to **lowest terms,** or simplest form, find the greatest common factor of the numerator and denominator and divide by that number.

$$\frac{3}{12} = \frac{1}{4}$$

The greatest common factor of 3 and 12 is 3.

$$\frac{3 \div 3}{12 \div 3} = \frac{1}{4}$$

To change a **mixed number** to a fraction greater than 1, multiply the denominator by the whole number and add the numerator. The denominator stays the same.

$$3\frac{5}{6} = \frac{23}{6}$$

To change a fraction greater than 1 to a mixed number, divide the denominator into the numerator. Put the remainder over the denominator.

$$\frac{16}{3} = 3\overline{)16}^{\,5\frac{1}{3}} \\ \quad\;\; \underline{15} \\ \quad\;\;\; 1$$

Finish Line Math–Level F

1 On Monday, there was $8\frac{1}{3}$ inches of snow. On Friday, there was $14\frac{1}{2}$ inches. How much snow fell from Monday to Friday?

A $5\frac{1}{2}$ inches   **C** $6\frac{1}{2}$ inches

B $6\frac{1}{6}$ inches   **D** $6\frac{5}{6}$ inches

> Did you choose B? That's correct. To subtract fractions with unlike denominators, change them to equivalent fractions by finding the lowest common denominator:
> $$14\frac{1}{2} = 14\frac{3}{6}$$
> $$-8\frac{1}{3} = 8\frac{2}{6}$$
> $$\overline{6\frac{1}{6}}$$

2 Howard ate $2\frac{1}{4}$ mini pan-pizzas. Marcia ate $3\frac{1}{4}$ mini pan-pizzas. How many mini pan-pizzas did they eat all together?

F 1   **H** $5\frac{1}{2}$

G $5\frac{1}{4}$ **J** $5\frac{3}{4}$

3 On an average day, 632 customers enter the museum. Approximately $\frac{1}{3}$ of them make a purchase. **About** how many people make a purchase on an average day?

A 200   **C** 250

B 225   **D** 400

4 Mr. Fodor drove $3\frac{3}{4}$ miles from school. He turned around and drove $1\frac{3}{8}$ miles to the deli. How far is the deli from school?

F $1\frac{3}{8}$ miles   **H** $2\frac{3}{8}$ miles

G $1\frac{3}{4}$ miles   **J** $2\frac{3}{4}$ miles

5 A recipe for bread calls for $\frac{3}{4}$ pound of whole wheat flour and $\frac{3}{4}$ pound of rye flour. How many pounds of flour is this all together?

A $\frac{6}{8}$ pound   **C** $1\frac{1}{2}$ pounds

B $1\frac{1}{4}$ pounds   **D** $1\frac{3}{4}$ pounds

6 A fruit shake calls for $5\frac{2}{3}$ ounces of pineapple and $2\frac{1}{3}$ ounces of coconut milk. How much more pineapple than coconut milk is used in this fruit shake?

F $3\frac{1}{6}$ ounces   **H** $7\frac{1}{6}$ ounces

G $3\frac{1}{3}$ ounces   **J** $7\frac{1}{3}$ ounces

7 Last summer, 11,726 people played golf at Putter's. About one-fourth of them were students. **About** how many students played at Putter's last summer?

A 2,000   **C** 4,000

B 3,000   **D** 5,000

8 For dessert, Kweisei's grandmother brought out $5\frac{1}{2}$ pies. When everyone had finished eating, there were $2\frac{3}{8}$ pies remaining. How many pies were eaten?

F $2\frac{1}{8}$ **H** $3\frac{1}{8}$

G $2\frac{1}{4}$ **J** $3\frac{3}{8}$

9 In one day, 273 people ate at Lynne's Luncheonette. About $\frac{1}{4}$ of those people ordered lemonade. **About** how many people had lemonade that day?

_____ _about 75 people_ _____

> To estimate the number of people who ordered lemonade, first round the number of people who went to the luncheonette to the nearest hundred: 273 rounds to 300. Then multiply to find how many ordered lemonade: $300 \times \frac{1}{4} = \frac{300}{1} \times \frac{1}{4} = \frac{300}{4} = 75$. About 75 people ordered lemonade.

10 Maxine picked $\frac{7}{8}$ of a pint of blueberries. Vivian picked $\frac{5}{8}$ of a pint of blueberries. What is the total amount of blueberries they have? Show your work. Express your answer in lowest terms.

_____

11 **About** how much is $\frac{5}{6}$ of 311? Show your work.

_____

12 Trees cover $8\frac{2}{3}$ acres of an $11\frac{3}{4}$-acre park. A lake covers the remaining acres. How many acres is the lake? Show your work.

_____

13 In a survey, 420 students were found to drink an average of $\frac{1}{4}$ gallon of milk per person each day. How many total gallons of milk do these students drink per day? Show your work.

_____

14 The chart shows the number of a certain DVD player sold by the salespeople at Electronic Alley in one month. Each salesperson earns $\frac{1}{8}$ of the price of the DVD player as a bonus for each DVD sold.

DVD SALES	
Salesperson	*Number Sold*
Jake	20
Eli	14
Barbara	26
Jules	12

$129^{00}

Part A

What is the total amount of money sold by each salesperson? Show your work.

Jake _____

Eli _____

Barbara _____

Jules _____

Part B

How much of a bonus did each salesperson earn? Explain how you found your answers.

_____

_____

_____

_____

_____

Ask yourself—

What is the price of one DVD player? How many DVD players did each salesperson sell?

Before you write—

Think about the operation you can use to find $\frac{1}{8}$ of the total each person sold.

Now—

Check your answer. Does it make sense?

3–R Computation and Numerical Estimation Review

Read each problem. Circle the letter of the best answer.

1 Maricella received a $50.00 gift certificate for Music Hut. She spent $23.69 on CDs. How much of her gift certificate does she have left?

A $25.41

B $26.31

C $26.41

D $27.31

2 Oscar jogged $\frac{7}{12}$ of a mile. Then he turned around and jogged $\frac{7}{12}$ of a mile home. How far did Oscar jog all together?

F $\frac{14}{24}$ mile

G $1\frac{1}{6}$ miles

H 0 miles

J $1\frac{4}{12}$ miles

3 Last week, Mom's Restaurant used 30.5 pounds of garlic. At that rate, how many pounds of garlic will Mom's use in 6 weeks?

A 180 pounds

B 183 pounds

C 210 pounds

D 213 pounds

4 Pam and her family went to a used book store. They bought 2 books that cost $4.35 each and 3 books that cost $3.75 each. How much did they spend on books all together?

F $8.70

G $11.25

H $19.95

J $20.45

5 Juan, Sophia, and Isaac built a model of the solar system for science class. The materials cost $56.35. If they each paid the same amount of money, **about** how much did each pay?

A $5

B $10

C $20

D $30

6 Yuri was keeping track of his protein intake. On Friday, he ate 17.5 grams of protein for breakfast, 22.4 grams for lunch, and 43.3 grams for dinner. **About** how many grams of protein did Yuri take in on Friday?

F between 81 and 82 grams

G between 82 and 83 grams

H between 83 and 84 grams

J between 84 and 85 grams

7 Which of these is the best estimate of $\frac{1}{5} \times 143$?

A 20

B 30

C 40

D 50

8 A roll of wrapping paper had $6\frac{2}{3}$ yards. Ben cut off $1\frac{1}{2}$ yards to wrap a present. How much paper remained on the roll?

F $4\frac{1}{3}$ yards

G $4\frac{1}{6}$ yards

H $4\frac{5}{6}$ yards

J $5\frac{1}{6}$ yards

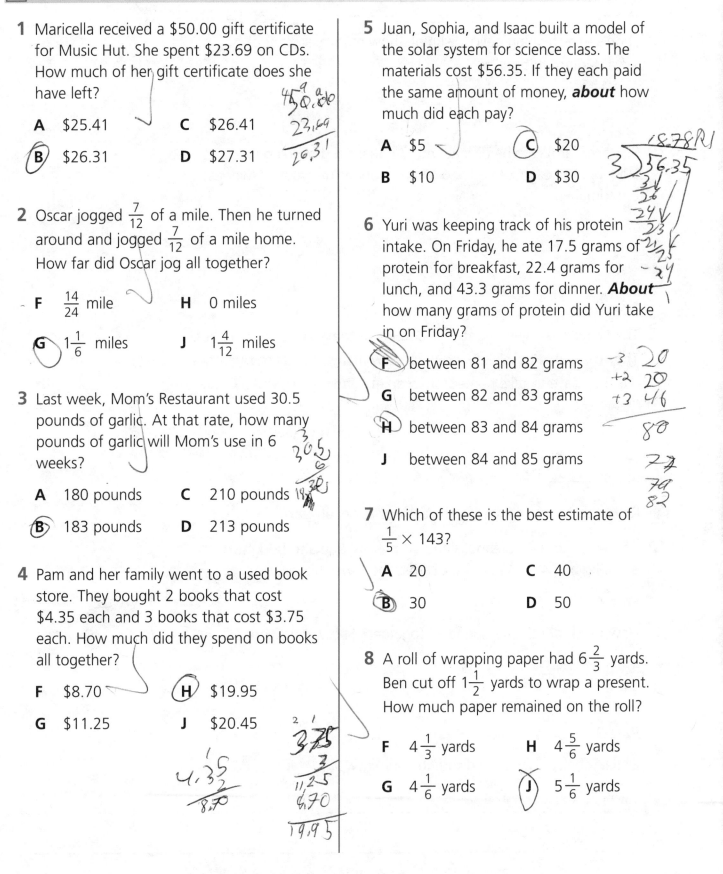

9 Last December, 631 customers bought handcrafted gifts at The Wood Shop. About $\frac{1}{9}$ of those people took advantage of the shop's free-shipping policy. Estimate how many people took advantage of this policy.

_____

10 A 5-acre farm is to be divided into 8 equal-sized building lots. How big will each lot be? Show your work. Write your answer as a decimal.

_____

11 The Schultz family brought $9\frac{7}{8}$ pounds of tomatoes to the market. They were able to sell $8\frac{2}{3}$ pounds. How many pounds of tomatoes did they have to take home from market? Show your work.

_____

Read the problem. Write your answer for each part.

12 Chanel bought 6 notebooks and 24 pencils. She also bought a stapler and 4 packs of index cards. There was no tax.

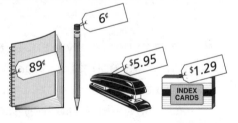

Part A

How much did Chanel spend all together? Show your work.

_____

Part B

Explain the steps you used to find your answer.

_____

_____

4–1 Units of Measurement

✹ Sometimes you need to change one measurement unit into another unit.

To change larger units to smaller units, multiply.

A picture frame is $\frac{1}{4}$ yard long. How many inches is that?

There are 36 inches in 1 yard.

$$\frac{1}{4} \times \frac{36}{1} = \frac{36}{4} = 9$$

The frame is 9 inches long.

To change smaller units to larger units, divide.

A table is 30 inches high. How many feet is that?

There are 12 inches in 1 foot.

$$30 \div 12 = 2\frac{1}{2}$$

The table is $2\frac{1}{2}$ feet high.

✹ Metric units of measurement are multiples of 10. You can use the shortcut of moving the decimal point when you multiply or divide to change one unit to another.

To change larger units to smaller units, multiply or move the decimal point to the right. Write as many zeros as you need.

A race is 50 kilometers long. How many meters is that?

There are 1,000 meters in 1 kilometer.

$$50 \times 1,000 = 50,000 \qquad 50. = 50,000$$

The race is 50,000 meters long.

To change smaller units to larger units, divide or move the decimal point to the left. Write as many zeros as you need.

A worm is 8 centimeters long. How many meters is that?

There are 100 centimeters in 1 meter.

$$8 \div 100 = 0.08 \qquad 008. = 0.08$$

The worm is 0.08 meter long.

Remember—

Inches (in.), feet (ft), yards (yd), and **miles (mi)** are customary units of length.

12 in. = 1 ft
36 in. = 1 yd
3 ft = 1 yd
5,280 ft = 1 mi

Ounces (oz) and **pounds (lb)** are customary units of weight.

16 oz = 1 lb

Cups (c), pints (pt), quarts (qt), and **gallons (gal)** are customary units of capacity.

2 c = 1 pt
2 pt = 1 qt
4 qt = 1 gal

Centimeters (cm), meters (m), and **kilometers (km)** are metric units of length.

100 cm = 1 m
1,000 m = 1 km

Grams (g) and **kilograms (kg)** are metric units of mass.

1,000 g = 1 kg

Milliliters (mL) and **liters (L)** are metric units of capacity.

1,000 mL = 1 L

Seconds, minutes, hours, and **days** are units of time.

60 seconds = 1 minute
60 minutes = 1 hour
24 hours = 1 day

Read each problem. Circle the letter of the best answer.

1 What is the equivalent of 40 centimeters in meters?

A 0.04 meter   **C** 4 meters

B 0.4 meter   **D** 400 meters

> Did you choose B? That's right. There are 100 centimeters in 1 meter. So move the decimal point to the **left** two places: 40 = 0.40 or 0.4 meter.

2 Aastha squeezed the juice from 3 grapefruits. What is the most likely amount of juice that Aastha got in all?

F 1 cup   **H** 1 gallon

G 4 cups   **J** 4 gallons

3 A seashell is 4 inches long. What fraction of a foot is that?

A $\frac{1}{5}$ foot   **C** $\frac{1}{3}$ foot

B $\frac{1}{4}$ foot   **D** $\frac{1}{2}$ foot

4 The Wilson family left New York City at 6:55 A.M. and arrived at Niagara Falls at 1:30 P.M. The Soong family left New York City at 7:05 A.M. and arrived at Niagara Falls at 3:55 P.M. How much longer did the trip take the Soong family than the Wilson family?

F 2 hours 5 minutes

G 2 hours 15 minutes

H 3 hours 10 minutes

J 3 hours 50 minutes

5 Ray put an apple on a scale. Which of these would most likely be the weight of an apple?

A 0.5 ounce   **C** 50 ounces

B 5 ounces   **D** 500 ounces

6 Use your inch ruler to help you solve this problem.

What is the length of the paper clip to the nearest $\frac{1}{8}$ inch?

F $1\frac{1}{2}$ inches   **H** $1\frac{3}{4}$ inches

G $1\frac{5}{8}$ inches   **J** $1\frac{7}{8}$ inches

7 How many cups hold the same amount of tomato juice as $1\frac{3}{4}$ quarts?

A 5 cups   **C** 9 cups

B 7 cups   **D** 11 cups

8 The scouts began their hike at 10:45 A.M. and set up camp 4 hours and 32 minutes later. At what time did the scouts set up camp?

F 3:07 P.M.   **H** 4:07 P.M.

G 3:17 P.M.   **J** 4:17 P.M.

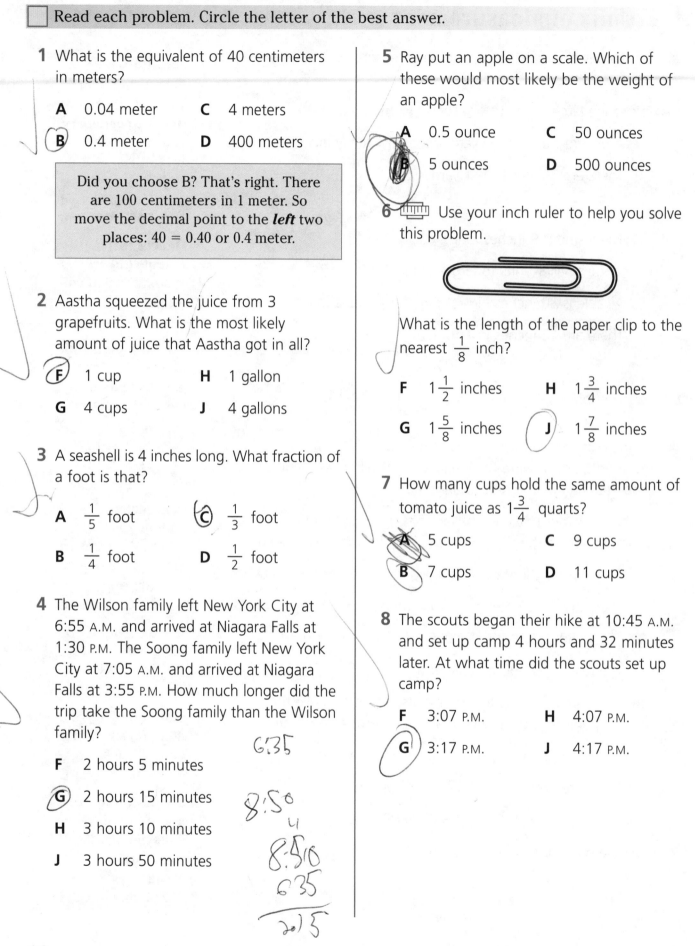

46

9 Minnie measured her elbow to wrist as 9 inches. What fraction of a foot is that?

$\frac{3}{4}$ *of a foot*

> There are 12 inches in 1 foot. To change smaller units to larger ones, divide: $9 \div 12 = \frac{3}{4}$. Nine inches is $\frac{3}{4}$ of a foot.

10 Use your centimeter ruler to help you solve this problem.

What is the length of the key to the nearest millimeter?

11 A train left Pennsylvania Station at 8:45 A.M. and arrived in Trenton, New Jersey, at 10:07 A.M. How long was the train ride? Show your work.

12 A bag of raisins weighs $\frac{1}{2}$ pound. If Sheila divides the raisins into 4 bags of equal size, how many ounces is each bag?

13 Express 79 grams as kilograms. Show your work.

14 Use your inch ruler to help you solve this problem.

The length of this watch's band is 5 times the longest distance across the face. How long is the watch band?

■ **Read the problem. Write your answer for each part.**

15 Rhea and Yaphet raced their pet turtles. Rhea's turtle won by traveling $1\frac{1}{2}$ yards in 3 minutes.

Part A

How far did Rhea's turtle travel in inches? Show your work.

_____

Ask yourself—
How many inches are in a foot? How many feet are in a yard?

Before you write—
Think about how to change minutes to seconds.

Part B

What was Rhea's turtle's average speed in inches per second? Show your work. Explain how you found your answer.

_____

_____

_____

_____

_____

_____

_____

_____

Now—
Check your answer. Does it make sense?

4–2 Perimeter and Area

✸ The **perimeter** of a figure is the distance around it.

To find perimeter, add the lengths of the sides.

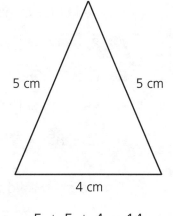

$$5 + 5 + 4 = 14$$

The perimeter of this triangle is 14 centimeters.

If the figure is a rectangle, you can multiply the length by 2 and the width by 2, and then add the products together.

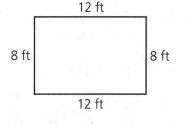

$$(2 \times 12) + (2 \times 8) = 24 + 16 = 40$$

The perimeter of this rectangle is 40 feet.

✸ The **area** of a figure is the number of square units inside it.

To find the area, count the number of square units.

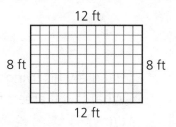

If the figure is a rectangle, you can multiply the length times the width to find the area.

$$12 \times 8 = 96$$

The area of this rectangle is 96 square feet.

Finish Line Math–Level F

Remember—

To find the perimeter of a **square,** multiply the length of a side by 4, since all the sides are equal.

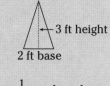

$$4 \times 2 = 8$$

To find the **perimeter** of a **rectangle,** multiply the length by 2 and the width by 2, then add the products.

$$P = (2 \times l) + (2 \times w)$$

Always express area in **square units,** such as:

square centimeters = cm^2

square inches = $in.^2$

square feet = ft^2

The **area** of a **square** or **rectangle** is the length times the width.

$$A = l \times w$$

The **area** of a **triangle** is one-half the base times the height.

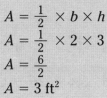

$$A = \frac{1}{2} \times b \times h$$
$$A = \frac{1}{2} \times 2 \times 3$$
$$A = \frac{6}{2}$$
$$A = 3 \text{ ft}^2$$

Read each problem. Circle the letter of the best answer.

1 The width of a pool is half its length. The pool is 25 meters long. What is its perimeter?

A 75 meters   **C** 150 meters

B 100 meters   **D** 200 meters

> Did you choose A? That's right. The pool's width is half its length. So the width is 25 ÷ 2, or 12.5 meters. Perimeter is twice the length plus twice the width: (2 × 25) + (2 × 12.5) = 75 meters.

2 Ralph has a table top that is 12 inches by 12 inches. He wants to put 1-inch square tiles on it. How many tiles will he need?

F 24   **H** 96

G 48   **J** 144

3  Use your centimeter ruler to help you solve this problem.

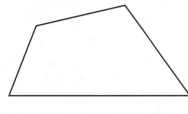

What is the perimeter of this figure?

A 6.5 cm   **C** 12.5 cm

B 10 cm   **D** 15 cm

4 A painting is 24 inches wide and 18 inches long. Which number sentence can Lois use to find the area of the painting?

F $18 + 24 = \square$

G $18 + 18 + 24 + 24 = \square$

H $18 \times 24 = \square$

J $18 \times 18 \times 24 \times 24 = \square$

5 Roberto's yard is 85 yards from side to side and 60 yards from front to back. Which of these choices should Roberto use to find the perimeter of his yard?

A $85 + 60 = \square$

B $(2 \times 85) + (2 \times 60) = \square$

C $85 \times 60 = \square$

D $(2 + 85) \times (2 + 60) = \square$

6 Tamara drew a figure on the grid below.

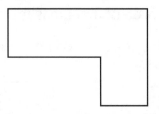

Which is the closest estimate of the area of the shape?

F 10 square units   **H** 20 square units

G 16 square units   **J** 24 square units

7  Use your inch ruler to help you solve this problem.

Hal drew his living room for a project. What is the area of the figure that Hal drew?

A 0.75 in.²   **C** 2.5 in.²

B 1.0 in.²   **D** 5 in.²

50

8 What is the area of the triangle?

<u>   96 yd²   </u>

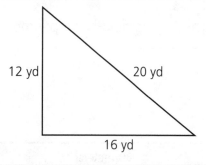

12 yd 20 yd

16 yd

> The formula for finding the area of a triangle is $\frac{1}{2} \times base \times height$. In this triangle, the base is 16 yards and the height is 12 yards. So $\frac{1}{2} \times b \times h = \frac{1}{2} \times 16 \times 12 = \frac{1}{2} \times 192 = 192 \div 2 = 96$. The area of the triangle is 96 yd².

9 ▱ Use your inch ruler to help you solve this problem.

Measure and label the sides of the figure. What is its perimeter? Show your work.

<u>   </u>

10 Lamont and Judy are putting a fence around a field that has a perimeter of 427 yards. They put up 85 yards of fence on Friday, 97 yards on Saturday, and 138 yards on Sunday. How much fence is remaining to be put up? Show your work.

<u>   </u>

11 ▱ Use your centimeter ruler to help you solve this problem.

What is the area of this figure? Show your work.

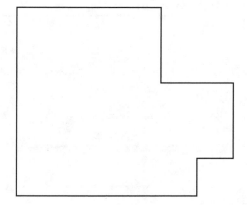

<u>   </u>

12 A rectangular playing field has a perimeter of 204 meters.

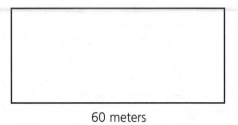

60 meters

Part A

What is the width of the field? Show your work.

_____

Part B

What is the area of the playing field? Explain how you found your answer.

_____

_____

_____

_____

_____

_____

Ask yourself—
How do I find the width if I know the perimeter and the length?

Before you write—
Think about the operation you use to find area.

Now—
Check your answer. Does it make sense?

4–3 Scale Drawings

✸ A **scale drawing** shows an object larger or smaller than it actually is. The **scale** tells what a unit in the drawing stands for in real life.

Look at this scale drawing. How many feet long is the boxcar?

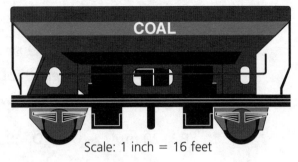

Scale: 1 inch = 16 feet

First, measure the drawing with an inch ruler.

The drawing is 3 inches long.

Then set up a proportion. Let f stand for the actual length in feet. Be sure the terms represent the same things on both sides of the proportion.

Length in drawing (inches) $\dfrac{1}{16} = \dfrac{3}{f}$ Length in drawing (inches)
Actual length (feet)   Actual length (feet)

Solve the proportion by cross multiplying:

$$1 \times f = 16 \times 3$$
$$f = 48$$

The actual boxcar is 48 feet long.

✸ If you know the actual size of an object, you can set up a proportion to find the scale used in a scale drawing.

A boxcar is 48 feet long. What is the scale used in the drawing?

Again, be sure the terms represent the same things on both sides of the proportion.

Length in drawing (inches) $\dfrac{1}{f} = \dfrac{3}{48}$ Length in drawing (inches)
Actual length (feet)   Actual length (feet)

$$1 \times 48 = f \times 3$$
$$\frac{48}{3} = f$$
$$16 = f$$

The scale used in the drawing is 1 inch = 16 feet.

Finish Line Math–Level F

Remember—
To solve a proportion, cross multiply.

When you cross multiply, you are multiplying the same units on each side.

in. × ft = in. × ft

When you divide to solve for the missing term, f, you are canceling out one of the units.

$$\frac{\cancel{\text{in.}} \times \text{ft}}{\cancel{\text{in.}}} = \text{ft}$$

The answer is in feet.

12 in. = 1 ft
3 ft = 1 yd

16 oz = 1 lb
2c = 1 pt
2 pt = 1 qt
4 qt = 1 gal

10 mm = 1 cm
100 cm = 1 m
1,000m = 1 km

1,000 g = 1 kg

1,000 mL = 1 L

Read each problem. Circle the letter of the best answer.

1 ▭ Use your inch ruler to help you to solve this problem.

The actual width of the fish is $7\frac{1}{2}$ inches. What is the actual length?

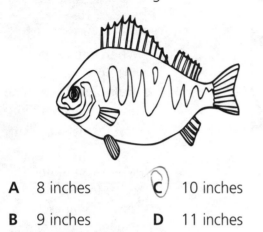

A 8 inches   C 10 inches

B 9 inches   D 11 inches

> Did you choose C? That's right. The width of the fish measures $1\frac{1}{2}$ inches. The real width is $7\frac{1}{2}$ inches. Divide to find the scale: $7\frac{1}{2} \div 1\frac{1}{2} = 5$, or the scale of 1 inch to 5 inches. The drawing measures 2 inches long. Its actual length is 2×5, or 10 inches.

▭ Use your inch ruler to help you solve this problem.

2 The actual length of the room is 32 yards. Which of the following is the scale used in the drawing?

[ ]

F 1 inch = 12 feet

G 1 inch = 24 feet

H 1 inch = 36 feet

J 1 inch = 48 feet

▭ Use your centimeter ruler and the diagram below to help you answer questions 3–5.

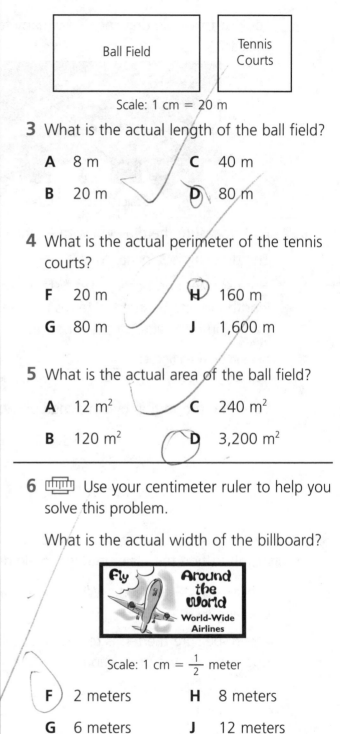

Scale: 1 cm = 20 m

3 What is the actual length of the ball field?

A 8 m   C 40 m

B 20 m   D 80 m

4 What is the actual perimeter of the tennis courts?

F 20 m   H 160 m

G 80 m   J 1,600 m

5 What is the actual area of the ball field?

A 12 m²   C 240 m²

B 120 m²   D 3,200 m²

6 ▭ Use your centimeter ruler to help you solve this problem.

What is the actual width of the billboard?

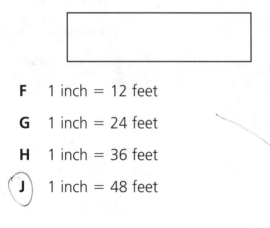

Scale: 1 cm = $\frac{1}{2}$ meter

F 2 meters   H 8 meters

G 6 meters   J 12 meters

54

Read each problem. Write your answer.

7 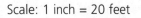 Use your inch ruler to help you solve this problem.

What is the actual area of the playground at Riverside Park?

___1,800 ft²___

Scale: 1 inch = 20 feet

> The formula for area is length × width. Measure the length and the width of the drawing: 3 inches long, $1\frac{1}{2}$ inches wide. Multiply by the scale, 1 inch = 20 feet, to find the actual measures: length = 20 × 3 = 60 feet, width = 20 × $1\frac{1}{2}$ = 30 feet. Then multiply the actual length and width to find the area: 60 × 30 = 1,800 ft².

 Use the diagram and your centimeter ruler to answer questions 8–10.

8 How far is Kyesha actually from the elm tree on the diagram of the field? Show your work.

_____

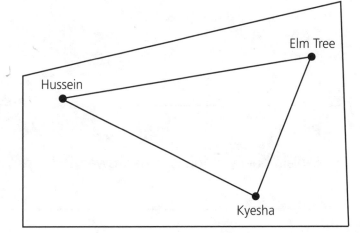

Scale: 1 cm = 6 m

9 What is the actual perimeter of the field? Show your work.

_____

10 What is the true area of the field? Show your work.

_____

11 ▭ Use your inch ruler to help you solve this problem.

The library is built in the shape of a U. The longest side is 48 feet long.

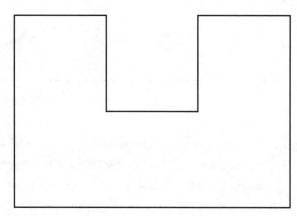

Part A

What is the scale used in the drawing? Show your work.

_____

Part B

Explain how you found your answer.

_____

_____

_____

_____

_____

Ask yourself—
How long is the drawing? How wide is it?

Before you write—
Think about the proportion you can use to find the scale.

Now—
Check your answer. Does it make sense?

4–R Measurement Review

Read each problem. Circle the letter of the best answer.

1 Use your inch ruler to help you solve this problem.

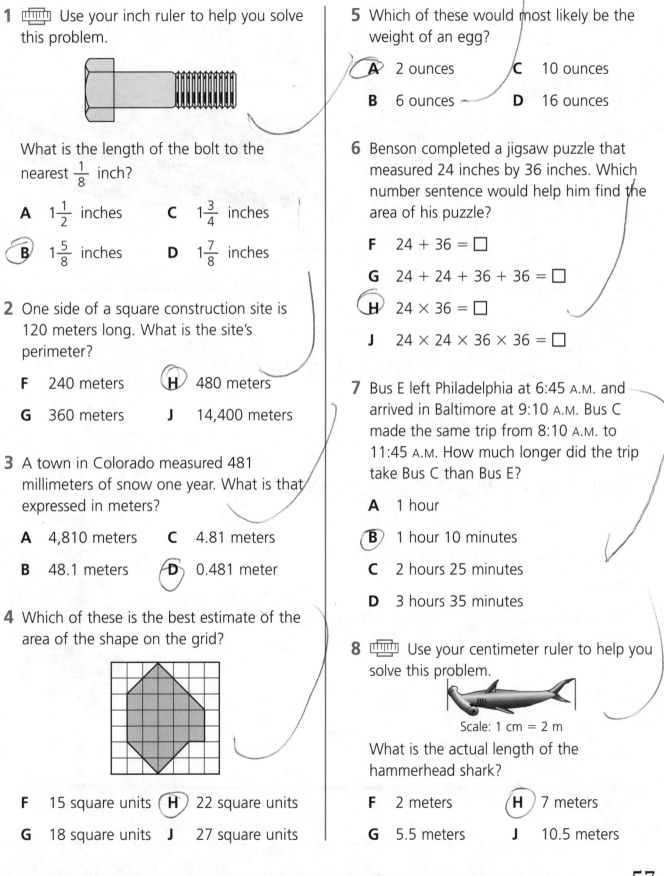

What is the length of the bolt to the nearest $\frac{1}{8}$ inch?

A $1\frac{1}{2}$ inches   C $1\frac{3}{4}$ inches

B $1\frac{5}{8}$ inches   D $1\frac{7}{8}$ inches

2 One side of a square construction site is 120 meters long. What is the site's perimeter?

F 240 meters   H 480 meters

G 360 meters   J 14,400 meters

3 A town in Colorado measured 481 millimeters of snow one year. What is that expressed in meters?

A 4,810 meters   C 4.81 meters

B 48.1 meters   D 0.481 meter

4 Which of these is the best estimate of the area of the shape on the grid?

F 15 square units   H 22 square units

G 18 square units   J 27 square units

5 Which of these would most likely be the weight of an egg?

A 2 ounces   C 10 ounces

B 6 ounces   D 16 ounces

6 Benson completed a jigsaw puzzle that measured 24 inches by 36 inches. Which number sentence would help him find the area of his puzzle?

F $24 + 36 = \square$

G $24 + 24 + 36 + 36 = \square$

H $24 \times 36 = \square$

J $24 \times 24 \times 36 \times 36 = \square$

7 Bus E left Philadelphia at 6:45 A.M. and arrived in Baltimore at 9:10 A.M. Bus C made the same trip from 8:10 A.M. to 11:45 A.M. How much longer did the trip take Bus C than Bus E?

A 1 hour

B 1 hour 10 minutes

C 2 hours 25 minutes

D 3 hours 35 minutes

8 Use your centimeter ruler to help you solve this problem.

Scale: 1 cm = 2 m

What is the actual length of the hammerhead shark?

F 2 meters   H 7 meters

G 5.5 meters   J 10.5 meters

9 How many inches are there in $\frac{2}{3}$ of a yard? Show your work.

_____

10 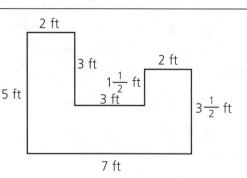 Use your inch ruler to help you solve this problem.

The actual length of the boat in the scale drawing is 35 feet long. What is the scale used in the drawing? Explain how you found your answer.

_____

_____

11 What is the area of this figure? Show your work.

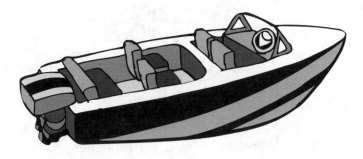

_____

Read the problem. Write your answer for each part.

12 Use your centimeter ruler to help you solve this problem.

The scale drawing shows a coast redwood tree.

Part A

What is the actual height of the tree? Show your work.

_____

Part B

Explain how you found your answer.

Scale: 1 cm = 10 m

_____

_____

58

5–1 Geometric Concepts

✳ An **angle** is formed by two rays or 2 line segments with the same endpoint. The rays or line segments are the sides of the angle. The endpoint is the **vertex,** or corner.

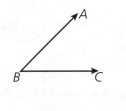

An angle is named by three points. The vertex is always the middle letter.

angle *ABC*   ∠*CBA*   angle *B*

A **right angle** measures 90°.

An **acute angle** measures **less** than 90°

An **obtuse angle** measures **more** than 90° and less than 180°.

✳ A **line** is a straight path with no endpoints. A line is named by any two points on it.

line *AB* $\overleftrightarrow{BA}$

Parallel lines never meet. They are always the same distance apart.

Perpendicular lines are intersecting lines that form right angles.

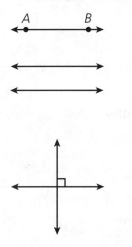

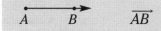
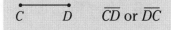
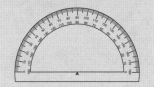

1 Which two lines on the basketball court are parallel?

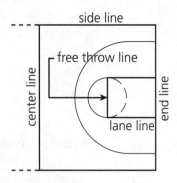

side line

free throw line

center line

end line

lane line

A center line and side line

B free-throw line and lane line

C free-throw line and end line

D lane line and end line

> Did you choose C? That's right. Parallel lines never meet, no matter how far they are extended. All the other choices meet at right angles, so they are perpendicular to one another.

2 What kind of angle measures 90°?

F acute

H right

G obtuse

J straight

Use this figure to answer questions 3–6.

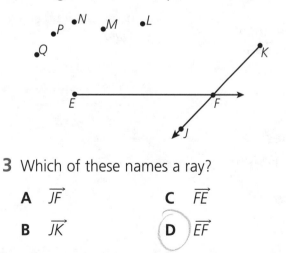

3 Which of these names a ray?

A $\overline{JF}$

C $\overrightarrow{FE}$

B $\overrightarrow{JK}$

D $\overrightarrow{EF}$

4 Through which point might a ray be drawn to form an acute angle at *E*?

F point *M*

H point *Q*

G point *N*

J point *P*

5 A line segment perpendicular to $\overline{JK}$ through point *F,* would most likely pass through which point?

A point *L*

C point *N*

B point *M*

D point *P*

6 Through which point might a ray be drawn to form an obtuse angle at *E*?

F point *K*

H point *N*

G point *M*

J point *P*

7 Use your protractor to answer this problem.

What is the degree measure of angle *A?*

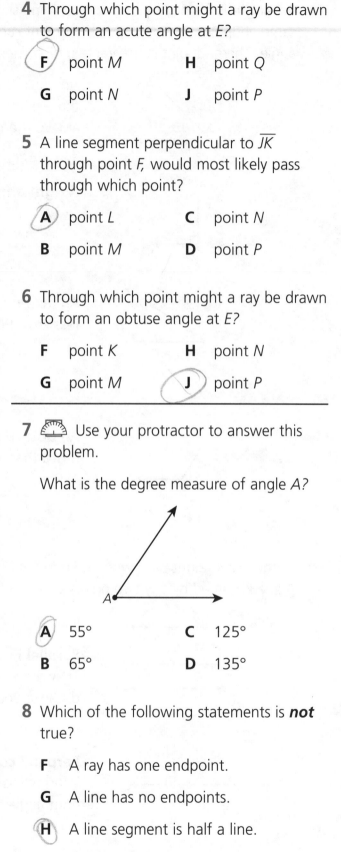

A

A 55°

C 125°

B 65°

D 135°

8 Which of the following statements is **not** true?

F A ray has one endpoint.

G A line has no endpoints.

H A line segment is half a line.

J Parallel lines never meet.

9 What kind of an angle will result if you add 45° to a right angle?

_____an obtuse angle_____

> Since a right angle measures 90°, adding 45° will result in an angle of 135°.
> An angle greater than 90° but less than 180° is an obtuse angle.

Use this figure to answer questions 10 and 11.

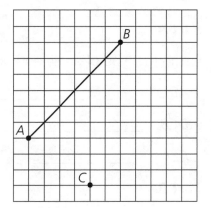

10 Draw line segment *CD* parallel to line segment *AB*.

11 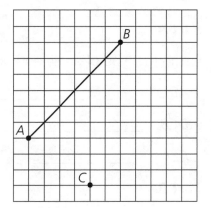 Use your protractor to help you solve this problem.
Draw a 35° angle at *A*, above line segment *AB*.

Use this figure to answer questions 12–14.

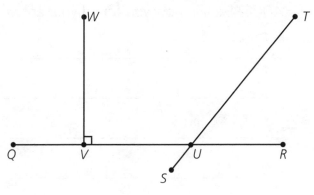

12 Name the line segment that is perpendicular to $\overline{VW}$.

_____

13 Name two acute angles.

_____

14 Use your protractor to help you solve this problem.

What would be the result if 55° were subtracted from the measure of ∠*TUV?*

_____

■ **Read the problem. Write your answer for each part.**

15 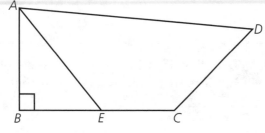 Use your protractor to help you solve this problem.

Part A

Name the type of angle and degree measurement for each.

∠ADC _____   ∠CBA _____

∠DCB _____   ∠BAD _____

∠CEA _____   ∠AEB _____

Part B

What is the sum of the measures of the angles of quadrilateral *ADCE?* Explain how you found your answer.

_____

_____

_____

_____

_____

_____

Ask yourself—
What type of angle measures less than 90°? More than 90°? Exactly 90°?

Before you write—
Think about how you find the sum of the measures of the angles of a triangle.

Now—
Check your answer. Does it make sense?

5–2 Plane Figures

✳ A **triangle** is a polygon with three sides and three angles. The sum of the angles is always 180°. Triangles are named for the kinds of angles or the number of equal sides they have.

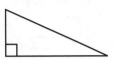 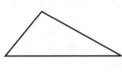

A right triangle
has 1 right angle.

An acute triangle
has 3 acute angles.

An obtuse triangle
has 1 obtuse angle.

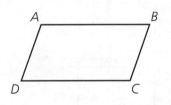 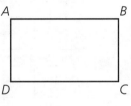 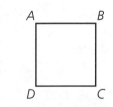

An isosceles triangle
has at least 2 equal sides.

A scalene triangle
has no equal sides.

A equilateral triangle
has 3 equal sides.

✴ A **quadrilateral** is a polygon with four sides. Some kinds of quadrilaterals have special names.

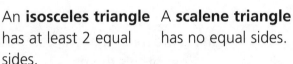

A parallelogram has opposite sides that are parallel and the same length.

A rectangle is a parallelogram with four right angles.

A square is a kind of rectangle. All four sides are the same length.

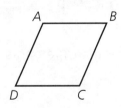 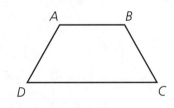

A rhombus is a kind of parallelogram. All four sides are the the same length.

A trapezoid has one pair of opposite sides that are parallel.

Finish Line Math–Level F

Remember—

A **polygon** is a closed plane figure formed by **line segments.** Each kind of polygon has a certain number of **sides** and **vertices,** or corners.

Polygons are named for the number of sides they have.

Name	Sides
Triangle	3
Quadrilateral	4
Pentagon	5
Hexagon	6
Octagon	8

A **regular** polygon has sides that are all equal in length. An **irregular** polygon has at least one side that is longer or shorter than the rest.

An **ordered pair** names the position of a point on a **coordinate grid.**

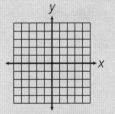

horizontal distance *or* distance left or right
↓
(3,2)
↑
vertical distance *or* distance up or down

Read each problem. Circle the letter of the best answer.

1 Which of these types of quadrilaterals can have exactly one pair of sides equal in length?

A rectangle   **C** trapezoid

B square   **D** parallelogram

> Did you choose C? That's correct. In a parallelogram, both pairs of opposite sides are equal in length. Rectangles are parallelograms. All 4 sides are equal on a square. Only a trapezoid could have one pair of equal sides.

2 Which best describes the figure below?

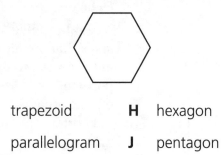

F trapezoid   **H** hexagon

G parallelogram   **J** pentagon

3 Which of these figures has at least one angle larger than a right angle?

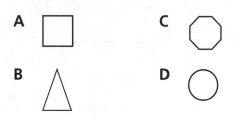

A   **C**

B   **D**

4 Which of these could be a true statement about a triangle?

F It may have more than 1 right angle.

G The sum of 2 sides is greater than the third side.

H It can have more than 1 obtuse angle.

J The sum of 2 sides is less than the third side.

5 Which of these quadrilaterals is a rhombus?

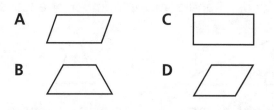

A   **C**

B   **D**

6 A triangle has angles that measure 65°, 50°, and 65°. What type of triangle is it?

F equilateral   **H** right

G obtuse   **J** acute

7 What are the coordinates that will complete the fourth corner of this rhombus?

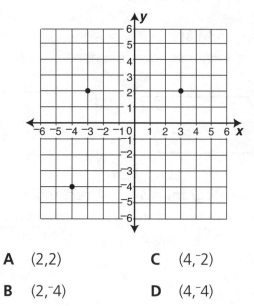

A (2,2)   **C** (4,⁻2)

B (2,⁻4)   **D** (4,⁻4)

8 Which could be a set of measurements for an isosceles triangle?

F 6cm, 6 cm, 6 cm

G 6cm, 4 cm, 6 cm

H 4cm, 4 cm, 8 cm

J 3cm, 4 cm, 5 cm

9 A closed figure has 8 angles of equal measure and 8 sides of equal length. What kind of a figure is it?

regular octagon

> A figure with 8 sides is an octagon. Since the question says that the angles are of equal measure and the sides are of equal size, it is a regular octagon.

10 A square is a polygon with many special features. List three other names that a square can be called.

_____

11 Gino has 24 inches of wire. If he folds it to make an equilateral triangle, how long would one side be? Why?

_____

12 Explain the difference between a trapezoid and a parallelogram.

_____

_____

13 Use the coordinate grid to answer this question.

Plot the points (4,2), (⁻5,3), and (⁻3,⁻2) on the grid.

Connect the points to make a triangle. Name the type of triangle you drew.

_____

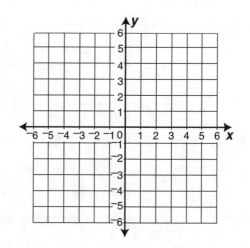

14 This diagram shows rectangle *ABCD*.

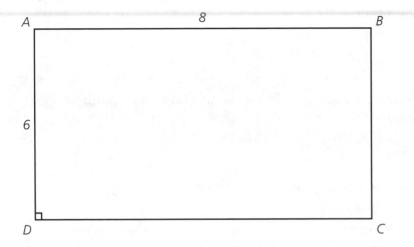

Part A

Draw a diagonal to separate the rectangle into 2 triangles. Classify the triangles by the number of sides and the kinds of angles.

_____

Part B

Explain how you know the types of triangles.

_____

_____

_____

_____

_____

Ask yourself—
How many equal sides do the triangles have? What could be the degree measure of the angles?

Before you write—
Think about the lengths of the sides of the triangles and the kind of angles they have.

Now—
Check your answer. Does it make sense?

5–3 Congruence and Symmetry

Remember—

Line segments and angles can also be congruent. Line segments must be the same length and angles must have the same degree measures to be congruent.

The symbol ≅ means *is congruent to.*

The symbol ~ means *is similar to.*

✷ **Congruent figures** have exactly the same size and shape. Congruent figures do not need to be in the same position. You can turn or flip a figure and it will still be congruent.

These figures are all congruent.

✷ **Similar figures** have the same shape, but they may be different sizes. The angles of similar figures are congruent, but the sides are in proportion to one another.

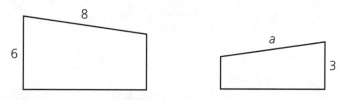

To find the length of an unknown side of a similar figure, set up a proportion with the corresponding sides of the figures and solve for the missing term.

$$\frac{8}{6} = \frac{a}{3}$$

$$8 \times 3 = 6 \times a$$

$$24 = 6a$$

$$\frac{24}{6} = \frac{6a}{6}$$

$$4 = a$$

Side *a* is 4 units long.

✷ A figure is **symmetrical** if it can be folded along a line to make halves that match exactly. A line of symmetry divides the figure into matching, or congruent, halves.

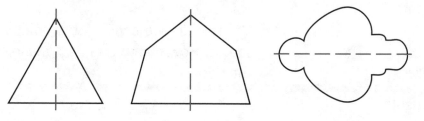

Some figures have **no** lines of symmetry.

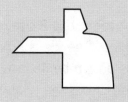

Some figures have **more** than 1 line of symmetry.

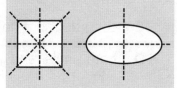

1 Which figure shows a line of symmetry?

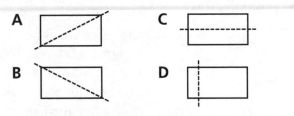

> Did you choose C? That's correct. Folding figures A, B, and D along the dashed line will not produce matching halves. Only figure C shows a line of symmetry with two equal halves.

2 Look at the triangle.

Which figure is congruent to the triangle above?

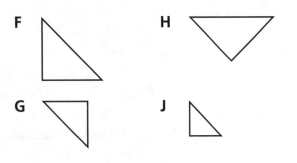

3 A room has 2 sizes of rectangular ceiling tiles. One tile is 20 cm by 30 cm. The other is 30 cm by 45 cm. Which statement best describes the relationship between the two tiles?

A similar but not congruent

B neither congruent nor similar

C congruent but not similar

D both similar and congruent

4 Which of these figures has **no** lines of symmetry?

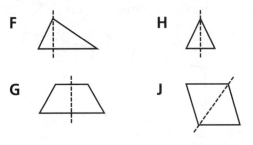

5 The triangles below are similar.

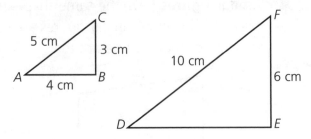

What is the length of side *DE*?

A 6 cm **C** 8 cm

B 7 cm **D** 9 cm

6 Which choice shows what the figure would look like reflected in a mirror?

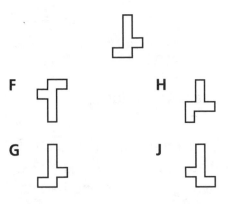

7 Shonelle drew every line of symmetry on a square. How many congruent triangles did she get?

A 4 **C** 8

B 6 **D** 12

8 Quadrilaterals *HIJK* and *CDEF* are similar.

How long is side *HK*?

_____9 inches_____

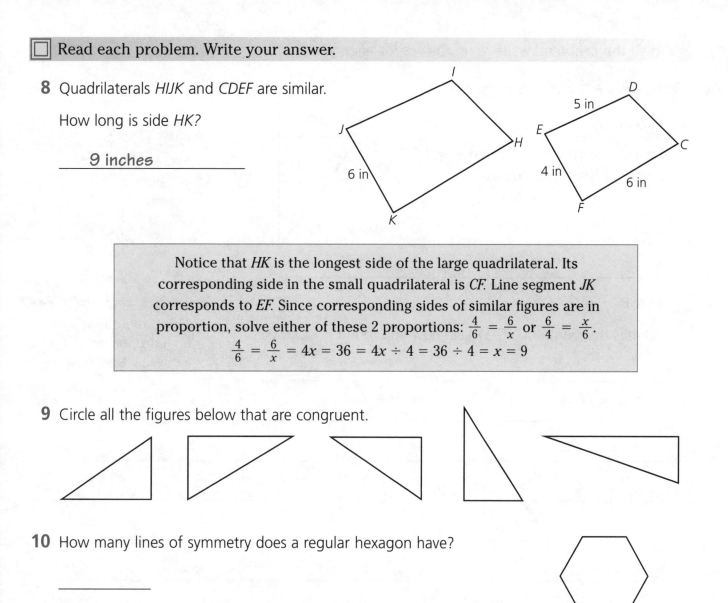

Notice that *HK* is the longest side of the large quadrilateral. Its corresponding side in the small quadrilateral is *CF.* Line segment *JK* corresponds to *EF.* Since corresponding sides of similar figures are in proportion, solve either of these 2 proportions: $\frac{4}{6} = \frac{6}{x}$ or $\frac{6}{4} = \frac{x}{6}$.

$\frac{4}{6} = \frac{6}{x} = 4x = 36 = 4x \div 4 = 36 \div 4 = x = 9$

9 Circle all the figures below that are congruent.

10 How many lines of symmetry does a regular hexagon have?

_____

11 Trapezoids *CDEF* and *LMNO* are similar.

What is the length of *LM*?
Show your work.

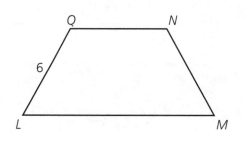

_____

12 What shapes are made if all of the lines of symmetry are drawn on this rhombus?

_____

13 Triangles *RST* and *RUV* are similar.

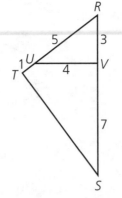

Part A

Identify the corresponding sides and angles of the two triangles.

Ask yourself—
What are similar figures? What sides and angles correspond?

_____

Part B

What is the length of *ST?* Explain how you found your answer.

Before you write—
Think about how to set up a proportion to find a missing term.

_____

_____

_____

_____

_____

_____

_____

Now—
Check your answer. Does it make sense?

5–R Geometry and Spatial Sense Review

Read each problem. Circle the letter of the best answer.

Use this diagram to answer questions 1 and 2.

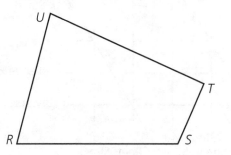

1 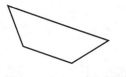 Use your protractor to answer this question.

What angle measures 75°?

A ∠U

C ∠S

B ∠R

D ∠T

2 Which sides of quadrilateral *RSTU* are perpendicular to each other?

F *RS* and *ST*

H *TU* and *ST*

G *RU* and *UT*

J *RU* and *ST*

3 Which best describes the figure below?

A pentagon

C parallelogram

B trapezoid

D rhombus

4 Which of the following statements is **not** true about a triangle?

F It can have 3 equal sides.

G It can have 2 perpendicular sides.

H It can have 1 obtuse angle.

J It can have 2 right angles.

5 Which of these pictures shows a line of symmetry?

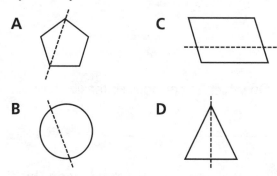

6 What is the lowest number of degrees that may be subtracted from a 132° angle to make it acute?

F 32°

H 43°

G 42°

J 90°

7 What figure can be described as a parallelogram with equal sides?

A trapezoid

C parallelogram

B rectangle

D rhombus

8 Look at this figure.

Which of these figures is congruent to the figure above?

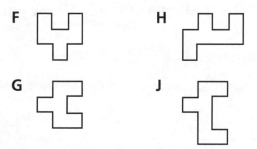

9 Rick lives on Elm Street. Hafez lives on a street that is parallel to Rick's.

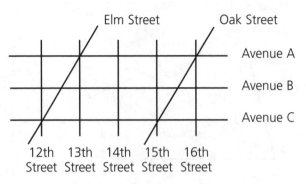

On which street does Hafez live?

_____

10 Draw all the lines of symmetry on this figure.

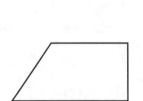

11 Explain what type of quadrilateral is pictured at the right and how you know.

_____

_____

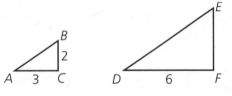

12 Triangles *ABC* and *DEF* are similar.

Part A

Which angle in *DEF* corresponds to ∠*A* in *ABC*?

_____

Part B

What is the length of side *EF*? Show your work.

_____

6–1 Data

✳ A **table** is an organized list of **data,** or information.

Gizmo does not shed. His fur keeps growing until it is cut. The table shows the length of Gizmo's fur as it was measured on the first day of each month.

GIZMO'S FUR	
Month	*Length in Inches*
December	1.4
January	1.8
February	2.3
March	2.6
April	3.0
May	0.2
June	0.6
July	1.0

You can use the data in a table to solve problems.

When was Gizmo's fur 3.0 inches long?

Read the table to find the answer.

Gizmo's fur was 3.0 inches long on April 1.

You can also use the data in a table to make a "guess" about something in the table that is not recorded.

About how long will Gizmo's fur be on September 1 assuming he does not get a haircut?

Gizmo's fur grows about 0.4 inch per month. In July, it measured 1.0 inch. Add 0.4 to find its length in August:

$$1.0 + 0.4 = 1.4 \text{ inches}$$

Then add 0.4 again to find its length in September:

$$1.4 + 0.4 = 1.8$$

Gizmo's fur will probably be 1.8 inches long.

Remember—
Each table consists of **rows** and **columns.**

FAVORITE FLAVORS	
Name	*Flavor*
Joe	Chocolate ← **Row**
Maggie	Vanilla
Yusef	Vanilla
Glen	Strawberry

↑
Column

The **range** of a set of data is the difference between the largest and smallest values.

3 7 11 15 16
The range of this set is
16 − 3, or 13.

The **mean** of a set of data is the average. To find the mean, add all the values. Then divide the sum by the number of values.

3 7 11 15 16
3 + 7 + 11 + 15 + 16 = 52
52 ÷ 5 = 10.4
The mean is 10.4.

Read each problem. Circle the letter of the best answer.

Use this table to answer questions 1–4.

SCHOOL LIBRARY USE	
Time	Number of Students
9 A.M.	20
10 A.M.	40
11 A.M.	12
12 P.M.	24
1 P.M.	35

1 Which is the best estimate of the number of students in the library at 12:30 P.M.?

A 20   C 35

B 30   D 40

> Did you choose B? That's correct.
> Since 12:30 P.M. is halfway between
> 12 P.M. and 1 P.M., the estimate should
> be halfway between 24 and 35.
> Subtract: 35 − 24 = 11, 11 ÷ 2 = 5.5 or
> about 6, 24 + 6 = 30.

2 At what time were the fewest students using the library?

F 9 A.M.   H 12 P.M.

G 11 A.M.   J 1 P.M.

3 What is the difference between the number of students using the library at 10 A.M. and those using it at 12 P.M.?

A 6   C 16

B 10   D 24

4 Of the 20 students in the library at 9 A.M., 15 were still there at 10 A.M. How many students came into the library between 9 A.M. and 10 A.M.?

F 5   H 25

G 20   J 35

Use this chart to answer questions 5–8.

SUMMER VACATIONS	
Place	Number of Students
Camping	97
Seashore	110
Amusement park	162
Other	53
Stayed home	94

5 Which is the best estimate of the total number of students surveyed?

A 300   C 700

B 500   D 900

6 What is the largest percent of students who could have visited Washington, D.C., on vacation?

F 10%   H 21%

G 18%   J 31%

7 How many more students went to an amusement park than stayed home?

A 39   C 68

B 52   D 110

8 Which of these statements can be concluded from the data in the chart?

F The most popular vacation destination was the seashore.

G Camping and amusement park made up more than half the vacations.

H More girls liked camping than boys.

J Students stayed home because they did not like the vacation choices.

74

Use this table to answer questions 9 –11.

9 The Schwartz family bought 1,000 gallons of heating oil on November 1. They saved $220 over what they would have had to pay to fill it on January 1. Which oil company did they buy from?

HEATING OIL (PRICE PER GALLON)		
Date	Heatz	Oilco
Nov. 1	1.27	1.25
Dec. 1	1.33	1.31
Jan. 1	1.45	1.47
Feb. 1	1.57	1.60
Mar. 1	1.57	1.57

_____Oilco_____

> First find the difference, or savings per gallon, in each oil company's prices for November and January: Heatz = $1.45 − $1.27 = $0.18, Oilco = $1.47 − $1.25 = $0.22. Then find the savings for 1,000 gallons: Heatz = 1,000 × $0.18 = $180, Oilco = 1,000 × $0.22 = $220. The family's oil company is Oilco.

10 What would have been the difference in cost for a customer to buy 550 gallons of oil from Oilco rather than Heatz when the difference in their prices was greatest? Show your work.

_____

11 Suppose heating oil prices moved higher and lower at the same rate each month. **About** what price would you expect Heatz' price per gallon to have been on January 15? Show your work.

_____

Use this chart to answer questions 12–14.

12 Change the tallies in the table to numerals. Write the number of pancakes in the last column of the table.

PANCAKE EATING CONTEST		
Contestant	Tally of Pancakes	Number
Leah	﷼ ﷼ ﷼ ﷼ ﷼ /	_____
Pete	﷼ ﷼ ﷼ ﷼ /	_____
Bette	﷼ ﷼ ﷼ ﷼ ////	_____
Yoshi	﷼ ﷼ ﷼ ﷼ ﷼ ﷼ ///	_____

13 Write one statement about the pancake eating contest that is supported by the data in the table.

_____

_____

14 Grapes cost $0.99 at Jay's Market in July. They went up
$0.45 per pound every month through November.
SuperSave had grapes for $0.89 in July. They went up
$0.50 each month.

Part A

Make a table using the data from above. Be sure to—
- give the table a title
- label each column with a heading
- record all the data

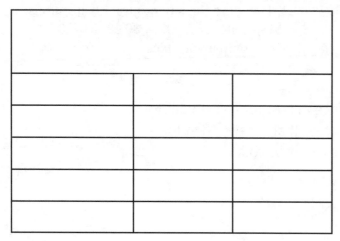

Part B

If the price of grapes continues to increase at the same rates at
both stores, how much of a difference will there be in a pound
of grapes between the two stores in January? Explain how you
know.

_____

_____

_____

_____

_____

Ask yourself—
What is the price of a
pound of grapes each
month from July
through November at
each store?

Before you write—
Think about the
operations you will
need to find the
January prices and to
compare the prices of
the two stores.

Now—
Check your answer.
Does it make sense?

6–2 Graphs

✹ The data from tables can also be shown in **graph** form.

BETSY'S MONEY	
Item	*Amount*
Clothes	$50.00
CDs	$20.00
Food	$10.00
Savings	$20.00

The table shows how Betsy spent her money.

✹ A **circle graph** shows the **parts of a whole.** The total must equal 100%.

BETSY'S MONEY = $100

In this graph, the size of the section compared to the whole is easy to see.

You can use a circle graph to solve problems.

How much did Betsy put in savings?

The total of the graph is $100. Add the totals given, and then subtract from 100:

$$50 + 20 + 10 = 80$$
$$100 - 80 = 20$$

She put $20 in savings.

✹ A bar graph uses bars to show data.

BETSY'S MONEY

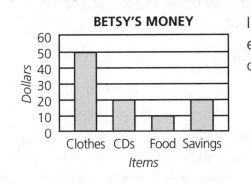

In this graph, the bars are easy to compare to each other.

Remember—

The **bars** on a bar graph stand for **numbers.** When a bar ends between numbers on the scale, it stands for the number that comes between.

MONTHLY SNOWFALL

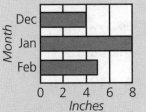

The bar for February stands for 5 inches.

A **double-bar graph** compares two sets of data.

CLASS SIZES, 1990 and 2000

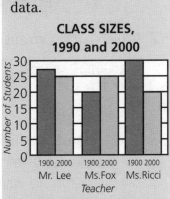

This double-bar graph compares class sizes in 1990 and 2000.

A **line graph** shows change over time.

TEMPERATURES IN MARCH

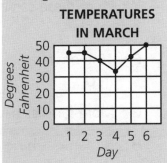

Read each problem. Circle the letter of the best answer.

Use this bar graph to answer questions 1–4.

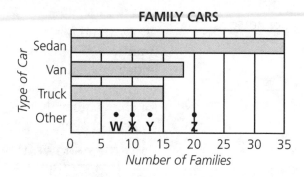

FAMILY CARS

1 How many more families have a sedan than a truck?

A 12   C 20

B 15   D 25

> Did you pick C? That's correct. A total of 35 families have a sedan. A total of 15 families have a truck. Subtract to find the difference: 35 − 15 = 20.

2 Which car do **about** 18 families have?

F sedan   H truck

G van   J other

3 The 13 families who have another type of car than those listed are not represented on the graph. To which point should the bar for Other be drawn?

A point W   C point Y

B point X   D point Z

4 Which of these can be concluded from the bar graph?

F 10 more families have a van than a truck.

G More families have vans than sedans.

H No families have a station wagon.

J Less than 100 families were surveyed.

Use this line graph to answer questions 5–8.

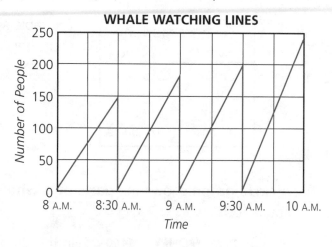

WHALE WATCHING LINES

5 Every time a boat arrives, everyone in line gets onto it, and a new line begins to form. How often does a boat arrive?

A every 15 minutes

B every 20 minutes

C every 25 minutes

D every 30 minutes

6 How many more people are on the 9:30 A.M. boat than on the 8:30 A.M. boat?

F 25   H 75

G 50   J 100

7 **About** how many people were in line for a boat at 9:15 A.M.?

A 100   C 150

B 125   D 175

8 Between 8:00 A.M. and 8:30 A.M., **about** how many people per minute joined the line?

F 5   H 15

G 10   J 20

78

□ **Read each problem. Write your answer.**

Use this circle graph to answer questions 9 and 10.

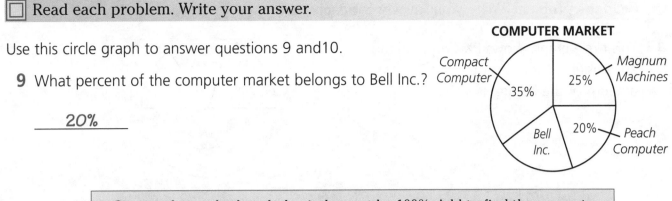

COMPUTER MARKET

9 What percent of the computer market belongs to Bell Inc.?

_____*20%*_____

> On a circle graph, the whole circle must be 100%. Add to find the percents listed: 35% + 25% + 20% = 80%. Then subtract the sum from 100 to find Bell's percentage: 100 − 80 = 20%.

10 How much more of the computer market do Magnum Business Machines and Peach Computer have together compared to Compact? Show your work.

_____

Use this line graph to answer questions 11 and 12.

11 Water freezes at a temperature of 32° Fahrenheit. On which days, if any, was the noon temperature at or below freezing?

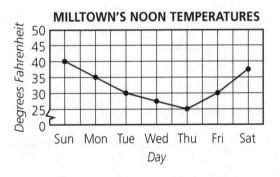

MILLTOWN'S NOON TEMPERATURES

_____

12 What is the range of noon temperatures for the period covered by the graph? Show your work.

_____

■ **Read the problem. Write your answer for each part.**

13 This circle graph shows PX Corporation's advertising budget for this year. The total amount of the budget is $100,000.

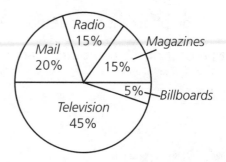

Part A

How much money was spent on each area? Show your work.

_____

Part B

Make a bar graph using the data you found above. Be sure to—

- give the bar graph a title
- label the scale and each bar
- record all the data

Ask yourself—

How do I change a percent to a decimal? What operation can I use to find the total spent on each area?

Before you write—

Think about the numbers you need to show on the scale.

Now—

Check your answer. Does it make sense?

6–3 Probability

✸ **Probability** is the chance that an event will happen. An **event** is also called an **outcome.**

> What is the probability of getting heads when tossing a coin?
>
> There are 2 possible outcomes to this event: heads or tails. There is only 1 favorable outcome: heads. So the probability of getting heads is 1 out of 2.

Each flip or pick is an **independent event.**

> If the coin is tossed a second time, the probability of landing on heads is still 1 out of 2.
>
> Paige has 2 red T-shirts and 3 white T-shirts in a drawer. If she picks one at random, what is the probability that it will be a white T-shirt?
>
> $$P(white) = \frac{3 \text{ (favorable outcomes)}}{5 \text{ (possible outcomes)}}$$
>
> The probability of picking a white T-shirt is 3 out of 5. If Paige picked from the same set again, the probability of picking a white T-shirt is still 3 out of 5.
>
> What is the probability of 2 people picking a white T-shirt from a set of 2 red shirts and 3 white shirts?
>
> $$P(white) \text{ and } P(white) = \frac{3}{5} \times \frac{3}{5} = \frac{9}{25}$$
>
> The probability of 2 people picking white shirts is $\frac{9}{25}$.

✸ Probability can be written as a fraction or as a decimal.

$$\frac{1}{2} = 0.5$$

This is the probability of 1 out of 2.

$$\frac{3}{5} = 0.6$$

This is the probability of 3 out of 5.

Remember—

An **event,** or outcome, is something that can happen, such as heads or tails when flipping a coin.

An event is **certain** if it definitely will happen. The probability that a number cube numbered 1 to 6 will land on a number from 1 to 6 is a certainty.

An event is **impossible** if it definitely will not happen. The probability that a number cube numbered 1 to 6 will land on 7 is an impossibility.

To change a fraction to a decimal, divide the numerator by the denominator.

$$\frac{3}{5} = 5 \overline{)\begin{array}{r} 0.6 \\ 3.0 \\ \underline{3\,0} \end{array}}$$

To change a decimal to fraction, put the decimal number over the place value of the digit in the rightmost column. Then reduce to lowest terms.

$$0.6 = \frac{6}{10} = \frac{3}{5}$$

---

1 Allison is going to flip a quarter 50 times. Which is the best estimate of the probability that all 50 flips will be heads?

A 0   **C** 0.5

B 0.25   **D** 1

Did you select A? That's right. The probability of getting heads is $\frac{1}{2}$, or 0.5. Multiply to find the probability of getting 2 heads in a row: $\frac{1}{2} \times \frac{1}{2} = \frac{1}{4}$, or 0.25. By the 8th flip, the probability is $\frac{1}{256}$, or 0.003906. By the 50th flip, the probability is even smaller. So 0 is a good estimate.

2 Yevgeny is going to spin the arrow 20 times in a row. How likely is it that the arrow will land on red all 20 times?

F It is certain that it will land on Red all 20 times.

G It will most likely land on Red all 20 times.

H It will most likely **not** land on Red all 20 times.

J It will definitely **not** land on Red all 20 times.

3 What is the probability of flipping a penny and getting 3 tails in a row?

A $\frac{1}{2}$ **C** $\frac{1}{6}$

B $\frac{1}{3}$ **D** $\frac{1}{8}$

4 A bag contains 12 tomatoes. Only 3 of the tomatoes are ripe. What is the probability of pulling a ripe tomato from the bag?

F $\frac{1}{3}$ **H** $\frac{1}{9}$

G $\frac{1}{4}$ **J** $\frac{1}{12}$

5 Margo's box has 6 green marbles, 6 red marbles, and 6 blue marbles. If she picks a marble from the box, what is the probability that it will be blue?

A $\frac{1}{18}$ **C** $\frac{1}{3}$

B $\frac{1}{6}$ **D** $\frac{1}{2}$

6 Students voted for their favorite swimming stroke. Six students chose backstroke, nine chose breaststroke, nine chose butterfly, and 12 chose freestyle. If one of these students is chosen at random, what is the probability that he or she chose butterfly?

F $\frac{1}{9}$ **H** $\frac{1}{4}$

G $\frac{1}{6}$ **J** $\frac{1}{3}$

7 A box has 10 mystery novels, 10 biographies, and 10 science fiction books. Edina reaches in the box and pulls out a mystery novel. Then she reaches in and pulls out another mystery. If she doesn't replace the books, what is the probability that Edina will pull out a mystery again?

A 1 out of 10   **C** 2 out of 7

B 3 out of 10   **D** 10 out of 30

8 The faces of this number cube are numbered 1 through 6.

If Alicea rolls the number cube 30 times, what is the best prediction of the number of times she will roll a 4?

_____5 times_____

> Each time Alicea rolls the cube there is a $\frac{1}{6}$ chance of rolling a 4. It makes no difference what the previous roll was; it's $\frac{1}{6}$ each time. Since the cube was rolled 30 times, $\frac{1}{6} \times 30 = \frac{30}{6} = 5$. The best prediction is that 5 rolls will result in the number 4.

9 Fred has a bag containing 18 blue rubber bands and 2 red ones. He reaches into the bag and pulls out a rubber band at random. Write a fraction that represents the probability that the rubber band Fred picked was blue.

_____

10 There are 3 pears and 4 apples in a bowl under a towel. Melanie reaches under the towel and randomly picks something from the bowl. What is the probability that she picked a piece of fruit?

_____

11 Justin attempted 75 free throws. What number of free throws did he have to make to get a probability of $\frac{2}{3}$? Show your work.

_____

12 In which set is there a higher probability of randomly selecting a triangle from the set of triangles and squares? Explain.

_____

_____

_____

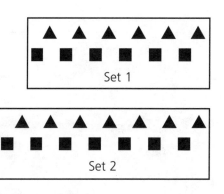

13 Use this diagram to help you solve the problem.

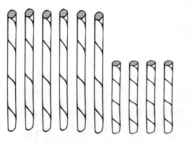

Part A

What is the probability of picking a long straw? Write your answer as a fraction in lowest terms and a decimal.

_____

Part B

Suppose a long straw was drawn from the set and **not** replaced. What is the probability that the next straw selected will be a long straw? Explain what is different from your answer to Part A.

_____

_____

_____

_____

_____

_____

_____

6–R Data Analysis, Statistics, and Probability Review

Read each problem. Circle the letter of the best answer.

Use this table to help you answer questions 1–3.

LUNCHMEAT PRICES	
Meat	*Price Per Pound*
Ham	$1.99
Turkey	$2.79
Roast Beef	$4.78
Bologna	$2.39

1 What is the order of the prices of lunch meat from greatest to least?

  A   roast beef, bologna, turkey, ham

  B   ham, bologna, turkey, roast beef

  C   roast beef, turkey, bologna, ham

  D   ham turkey, roast beef, bologna

2 Which two lunch meats together cost the same as a pound of roast beef?

  F   bologna and ham

  G   ham and turkey

  H   turkey and bologna

  J   roast beef and ham

3 Which of the following is the most likely graph of the data in the table?

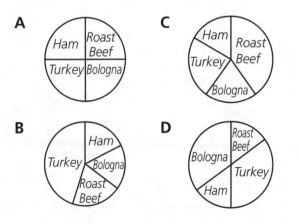

Use this graph to answer questions 4–5.

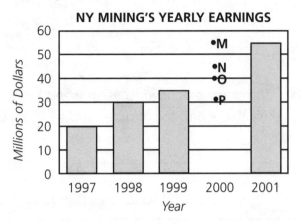

4 NY Mining's earnings were $45 million in 2000. Which point marks where the top of the bar for that year should be drawn?

  F   point M   **H**   point O

  G   point N   **J**   point P

5 *About* how much would you expect NY Mining to earn in 2002?

  A   between $30 and $40 million

  B   between $40 and $50 million

  C   between $40 and $50 million

  D   between $60 and $70 million

6 A sack contains 5 green cubes, 4 red cubes, and 3 blue cubes. If a monkey reaches in and pulls out one cube, what is the probability that it will be a red cube?

  F $\frac{1}{4}$ **H** $\frac{5}{12}$

  G $\frac{1}{3}$ **J** $\frac{1}{2}$

Read each problem. Write your answer.

Use this line graph to answer questions 7 and 8.

DUCKS AT WALDEN POND

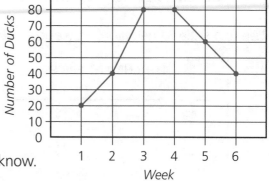

7 In which 2 weeks did Maria and José count 40 ducks?

_____

8 If the graph extended to a 7th week, what would most likely happen to the number of ducks? Explain how you know.

_____

_____

9 Which two items account for more than half of Mike's allowance money?

_____

MIKE'S ALLOWANCE MONEY

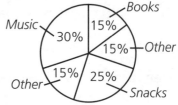

Read the problem. Write the answer for each part.

10 Miho took inventory of her clothing.

Part A

What fraction of Miho's clothes are pants?

_____

Part B

Make a bar graph to show the data in this table.
Be sure to—

- give the bar graph a title
- label the scale and each bar
- record all the data

MIHO'S CLOTHING INVENTORY	
Item	_Number_
Shirts	15
Pants	6
Shorts	9
Sweaters	5

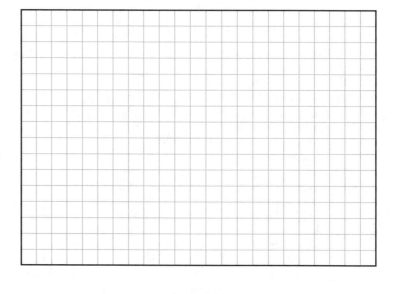

7–1 Patterns

✹ To find a **pattern** in a sequence of numbers, look at the numbers in order and decide how they change. The change can be described by a **rule.**

What number comes next in the pattern?

3, 6, 9, 12, 15, ___?___

Each number is 3 more than the previous number. So the rule is "add 3." To find the next number, add 3 to the last number:

15 + 3 = 18

The next number will be 18.

✹ To find a **geometric pattern** in a sequence of figures, look at the shapes. Find where the shapes or the position of a shape repeats.

The figures repeat themselves after four figures. The missing figure is ◣ .

✹ Some patterns combine geometric elements and numbers.

```
                        ☆ ☆ ☆ ☆
                        ☆ ☆ ☆ ☆
        ☆ ☆    ☆ ☆ ☆ ☆    ☆ ☆ ☆ ☆
☆ ☆    ☆ ☆    ☆ ☆ ☆ ☆    ☆ ☆ ☆ ☆    ___?___
```

Each group of stars increases by 2 times the previous group. The rule for this pattern is "multiply by 2." The next group will have 2 × 16 , or 32 stars.

Read each problem. Circle the letter of the best answer.

A collector arranged marbles in a row of boxes.

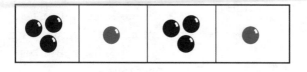

1 The row has 12 boxes in all. How many red marbles are in the row?

A 3   **C** 12

B 6   **D** 18

> Did you choose B? That's correct.
> There is a red marble in 2 of the boxes
> shown. Continuing the pattern to 12
> boxes will show 4 more red marbles:
> 2 + 4 = 6.

2 Which rule can be used to find the next number in this pattern?

270, 90, 30, 10, __?__

F multiply by 3   **H** divide by 3

G divide by 2   **J** subtract 60

3 Olivia is using this design of tiles on a tabletop.

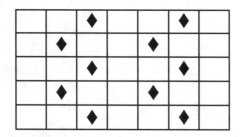

When the table is finished, there will be 105 squares. How many squares will have diamonds?

A 30   **C** 40

B 35   **D** 45

4 Which rule can be used to find the next number in the pattern?

2, 10, 42, 170, __?__

F add 2, then multiply by 2

G add 4, then multiply by 2

H multiply by 4, then add 2

J multiply by 2, then add 4

5 Look at the pattern below.

If the pattern continues, how many triangles will there be in Figure 6?

A 19   **C** 23

B 21   **D** 25

6 What number comes next in this sequence?

4, 6, 10, 18, 34, __?__

F 62   **H** 95

G 66   **J** 101

7 Look at the pattern.

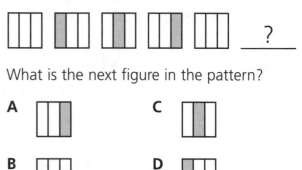

What is the next figure in the pattern?

A   **C**

B   **D**

8 What is the ninth number in this series?

2, 9, 16, 23, 30, ...

_____58_____

> The rule for this pattern is "add 7." Multiply the rule number by 9: $7 \times 9 =$ 63. Then subtract the difference between the rule number 7 and the first number in the sequence $(7 - 2 = 5)$: $63 - 5 = 58$. The ninth number is 58.

9 What are the next **two** numbers in this pattern? Show your work.

100, 10, 1, 0.1, __?__, __?__

_____

10 Name the rule that can be used to find the next number in the pattern.

5, 8, 14, 26, ...

_____

11 A jeweler has arranged boxes of round, square, and oval gems in a display case.

What shape gem will be in the 23rd box in the case? Explain how you know.

_____

_____

12 A number pattern begins with 8. It triples the number and then subtracts 7. What is the fifth number in the pattern? Show your work.

_____

13 Look at the pattern below.

Part A

Draw the next figure in the pattern.

Part B

Suppose the pattern keeps repeating. Which pattern will be in the 137th position? Explain how you found your answer.

_____

_____

_____

_____

_____

_____

Ask yourself—
How many figures are there until the pattern repeats?

Before you write—
Think about how to divide the number of figures in the pattern into 137 evenly.

Now—
Check your answer. Does it make sense?

7–2 Functions

✳ A **function** is a mathematical relationship between two numbers. The value of the first, or **input,** number determines the value of the second, or **output,** number.

A function can be shown as an **input-output table,** also called a **function table.**

What is the rule for this IN-OUT table?

IN	OUT
1	8
2	9
3	10
5	12

In this table, the number in the OUT column is always 7 more than the number in the IN column. The rule is "add 7."

✳ A function can also be described in a word problem.

All items at Martin's Furniture are $25 off the original price. If a table originally costs $145, what is its sale price?

First, determine the rule. The problem says all items are $25 off. That means "subtract 25." Then find the sale price by subtracting:

$$145 - 25 = 120$$

The sale price of the table is $120.

✳ Sometimes a rule can have more than one step.

IN	OUT
1	5
3	9
5	13

What is the rule?

The IN number is multiplied by 2 and then 3 is added.

Remember—

If you know the rule of a function, you can find any OUT number given an IN number.

The rule is "multiply by 6."
What will be the result if 9 is the IN number?
$6 \times 9 = 54$
The OUT number is 54.

If you know the rule and the OUT number, use the inverse and work backwards to find the IN number.

The rule is "subtract 2." So the inverse is "add 2."
What is the IN number if the OUT number is 11?
$11 + 2 = 13$
The IN number is 13.

Read each problem. Circle the letter of the best answer.

1 Hannah is using a rule to change IN numbers to OUT numbers.

What is the missing number in this table?

IN	OUT
3	12
7	16
4	13
?	21

A 5   **C** 12

B 9   **D** 13

> Did you choose C? That's correct. First find the rule by finding the difference between each IN and OUT number, 9. So the rule is "add 9." To find the missing number, use the inverse operation: $21 - 9 = 12$.

2 What rule is being used to change the IN number to an OUT number?

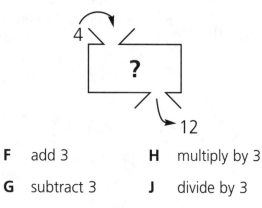

F add 3   **H** multiply by 3

G subtract 3   **J** divide by 3

3 Emma wrote a computer program that multiplies a number by 5 and then subtracts 3. If she puts 9 into the program, what number will she get back?

A 27   **C** 37

B 32   **D** 42

4 What is the missing number in this table?

IN	OUT
54	6
27	3
81	9
45	?

F 4   **H** 6

G 5   **J** 7

5 What rule does this table show?

IN	OUT
3	0
4	6
5	12

A add 3, then multiply by 6

B subtract 3, then multiply by 6

C add 6, then multiply by 3

D subtract 6, then multiply by 3

6 If you hand Felix a 3, he will change it to 11. He changes 0 to 2 and 5 to 17. What number would Felix change to 26?

F 4   **H** 8

G 6   **J** 9

7 Tim is going to subtract 7 from any number he is given and then multiply the result by 5. Dana tells Tim she knows a different rule that will give exactly the same results. What is Dana's rule?

A multiply by 5, then subtract 7

B multiply by 7, then subtract 35

C multiply by 7, then subtract 5

D multiply by 5, then subtract 35

8 A florist puts a certain number of carnations in every flower arrangement. If an arrangement has 15 flowers, 5 of them are carnations. If it has 24 flowers, 8 are carnations. What rule does the florist use to determine how many carnations go in each arrangement?

___divide by 3___

> To figure out how many "in each," use division. Divide the total number of flowers in each arrangement by the number of carnations in it: $15 \div 5 = 3$, $24 \div 8 = 3$. The rule the florist uses is to divide the total flowers in the arrangement by 3.

9 This function machine changes IN numbers to OUT numbers.

What rule is being used?

_____

$$60 \rightarrow \boxed{?} \rightarrow 6$$
$$40 \rightarrow \phantom{\boxed{?}} \rightarrow 4$$

10 Mr. Grove buys used appliances. He cleans them up and replaces old parts. Then he sells them for double what he paid. He bought a stove for $45 and a dishwasher for $57. How much would he sell these appliances for?

_____

11 A classified ad in the local paper costs $6.00 for the first 20 words and $0.20 for each additional word. How much would it cost to run a 31-word ad? Show your work.

_____

12 The table shows the cost of parking at a certain parking meter.

Fill in the missing numbers.

PARKING METER COSTS	
Price	*Time in Minutes*
$0.50	30
$0.75	45
	75
$3.50	

■ Read the problem. Write your answer for each part.

13 There is a sale at a sporting goods store.

STORE PRICES		
Item	*Regular Price*	*Sale Price*
Baseball glove	$ 60	$45
Football	$ 40	$30
Snowboard	$150	?
Ski Jacket	?	$60

Part A

What is the rule used to change the regular prices to sale prices?

_____

Part B

Find the missing prices. Explain how you found your answers.

_____

_____

_____

_____

_____

_____

7–3 Number Sentences

✴ An **expression** is a name for a number.

$$12 \qquad 6 + 8 \qquad \frac{15}{3} \qquad q + 4$$

An expression can be only a number, or it can contain numbers, letters, and operations. A letter that stands for a number is called a **variable.**

✴ An **equation** is a number sentence that says two things are equal. The sides of an equation are in balance.

$$7 + 5 = 6 + 6$$

$$7 + 5 = 12 \text{ and } 6 + 6 = 12$$

$$\text{So } 7 + 5 = 6 + 6 \text{ because } 12 = 12.$$

To solve an equation, "undo" the operations by using the inverse operation on both sides. Use a box or a variable to stand for the missing number.

$$5n = 15$$
$$\frac{5n}{5} = \frac{15}{5}$$
$$n = 3$$

✴ An **inequality** is a number sentence comparing two things. It says one thing **is greater than** or **is less than** something else.

Solve an inequality the same as you would an equation.

$$5 + n < 10$$

$$5 - 5 + n < 10 - 5$$

$$n < 5$$

Any number that is less than 5 will make this inequality true.

$$n = 0, 1, 2, 3, 4$$

$$5 + 0 < 10$$

$$5 < 10$$

$$5 + 1 < 10$$

$$6 < 10$$

Finish Line Math–Level F

Remember—

You can use any letter to stand for a **variable.**

$$w = \text{width}$$
$$l = \text{length}$$
$$d = \text{distance}$$

Some words give clues about operations.

Divided among or **split equally** signals division.

Total, in all, or **all together** signals addition or multiplication.

Less than or **difference** usually signals subtraction.

The symbol $>$ means *is greater than.*

$$6 + 5 > 9$$

The symbol $<$ means *is less than.*

$$10 - 3 < 9$$

1 What number could go in the box to make this number sentence true?

$$35 - \square < 25$$

A 5   **C** 10

B 8   **D** 12

> Did you select D? That's right. Test all the answers. Subtract 5 or 8 from 35 and the answer would be greater than 25. Subtracting 10 would give an answer equal to 25. That leaves $35 - 12 = 23$, which is **_less than_** 25.

2 Which expression could represent a number more than 23?

F $23 - n$ **H** $23 \div n$

G $n - 23$ **J** $n + 23$

3 What number goes in both boxes to make this number sentence true?

$$\square \times 5 = \square \times 3 + 12$$

A 0   **C** 6

B 4   **D** 8

4 Which choice will make this inequality a true statement?

$$25 - \square > 15$$

F any number greater than 10

G any number less than 10

H any number greater than 15

J any number less than 15

5 Which expression says 5 less than twice a number?

A $5n - 2$ **C** $5 - 2n$

B $2n - 5$ **D** $2 - 5n$

6 Miriam bought some postcards for 35 cents each. She bought 6 more than the other cards for 25 cents each. She spent $5.10 in total. If p stands for the number of 35-cent postcards, which equation could you use to find how many postcards Miriam bought at each price?

F $35(p + 6) + 510 = 25p$

G $25p + 35(p + 6) = 510$

H $35p + 25(p + 6) = 510$

J $25(p + 6) - 510 = 35p$

7 Which number could go in the box to make the number sentence true?

$$\square \times 7 - 6 > 47$$

A 5   **C** 7

B 6   **D** 8

8 Henry took a taxi to the train station. The rate was $6 for the first mile and $1.25 for each additional mile. He gave the driver $16.75. Which equation can be used to find d, the length of Henry's trip?

F $d = 6 + \frac{16.75}{1.25}$

G $1.25d = 10.75$

H $d = \frac{16.75}{1.25} - 6$

J $d = \frac{16.75}{1.25}$

9 At the ballpark, Marguerita bought 2 hot dogs and 3 bags of peanuts. Hot dogs cost $0.50 more than peanuts. All together, Marguerita spent $11. Write an equation that can be solved to find the cost of a hot dog.

$3p + 2(p + \$0.50) = \$11.00$

> Let p stand for the cost of a bag of peanuts. Marguerita spent $3p$ on peanuts. Since hot dogs were 50 cents more than peanuts, she spent $2(p + \$0.50)$ on hot dogs. Finally, put it together to show what she spent on hot dogs and peanuts: $3p + 2(p + \$0.50) = \$11.00$.

10 Write an expression that means 8 less than 4 of a number, n.

11 In the inequality below, the same number must go in each box.

$$5 \times \square < 15 + \square$$

What set of numbers can go in the boxes to make the inequality true?

12 A car travels for 6 hours at 65 miles per hour. Write an equation to find d, the distance the car traveled.

13 An elevator can hold less than 2,500 pounds. The people currently on the elevator weigh 1,000 pounds. Write an inequality for the additional number of pounds, p, that the elevator can hold.

Read the problem. Write your answer for each part.

14 Martin bought a deck of cards for c dollars and a book of card tricks. The book cost $5.00 more than the deck of cards. He paid a total of $12.00.

Part A

Write an equation that can be used to find the cost of a deck of cards.

_____

Part B

Solve the equation and then explain how you can find the cost of the book.

_____

_____

_____

_____

_____

_____

Ask yourself—
If c equals the price of the deck of cards, what expression represents the price of the book?

Before you write—
Think about how to solve equations and what operation you can use to find the cost of the book.

Now—
Check your answer. Does it make sense?

7–R Patterns, Functions, and Algebra Review

☐ Read each problem. Circle the letter of the best answer.

1 Which of these rules can be used to find the next number in the pattern?

100, 48, 22, 9, …

A divide by 4, then add 23

B divide by 2, then subtract 2

C multiply by 2, then subtract 2

D multiply by 4, then subtract 23

2 Inez has 3 more than twice as many scarves as her friend, Kara. Together, they have 15 scarves. Suppose c stands for the number of scarves that Kara has. Which equation could you use to find the number of scarves each girl has?

F $c + (3 \times c) + 2 = 15$

G $c + (2 + c) \times 3 = 15$

H $c + (2 \times c) + 3 = 15$

J $c + (3 \times c) + 2 = 15$

3 A certain function machine subtracts 5 from a number and then multiplies the result by 7. Which choice shows what this function would do to the number 9?

A 28   **C** 68

B 38   **D** 98

4 If the pattern below continues for 16 figures, how many pentagons will there be?

□	△	⬠	□	△	⬠

F 4   **H** 6

G 5   **J** 7

5 What rule did Sammy use to change each IN number to the OUT number?

IN	OUT
2	2
3	5
4	8
5	11

A add 8, then add 1

B add 3, then multiply by 4

C multiply by 4, then add 3

D multiply by 3, then subtract 4

6 What numbers will make this inequality true?

$21 - \square < 15$

F all numbers greater than 6

G all numbers between 0 and 6

H all numbers less than 6

J all numbers

7 Which is the next number in the pattern?

2, 3, 5, 8, 12, …

A 17   **C** 21

B 19   **D** 23

8 Which choice makes this number sentence true?

$8 \times \square - 7 = 41$

F 4   **H** 8

G 6   **J** 10

Read each problem. Write your answer.

9 What are the next two numbers in this number pattern?

1, 9, 33, 105, …

_____

10 If the pattern below is repeated, what will be the 86th figure? Explain how you figured it out.

_____

_____

11 Max left home and drove north for 4 hours at 65 miles per hour. He met with a client. Then he drove south at 55 miles per hour for 3 hours. Write an equation that can be solved to find how far Max drove in miles, *m*.

_____

Read the problem. Write your answer for each part.

12 All winter clothes at Logan's are $\frac{1}{4}$ off the regular price. Then, half is taken off the marked-down price at the register.

Part A

Write an equation that can be used to find *f,* the final price of clothes. Let *p* stand for the regular price. What is the final price of a jacket with a regular price of $120? Show your work.

_____

Part B

Explain how to find the regular price of a sweater that had a final sale price of $30.

_____

_____

8–1 Problem Solving

✳ Sometimes there is more information in a problem than is needed to solve the problem. **Extra information** is known as **irrelevant** or unnecessary information. You can ignore irrelevant information in a problem.

> Julius and Caroline drove to visit their grandmother. They left at 8:30 A.M. and drove for 3 hours at 60 miles an hour. How far away was their grandmother's house?

> To find how far away their grandmother lived, you need to know how long they drove and how fast. You do not need to know the time they left.

✳ Sometimes information is **missing.**

> Mrs. Osborne bought dried flowers for her living room. Each flower cost $3. How much did she pay all together?

> To answer this problem, you need to know how many flowers Mrs. Osborne purchased.

✳ Sometimes information is **hidden** in the problem.

> Fran bought a dozen pairs of socks at $4 a pair, a pair of pants for $35, and 2 sweatshirts for $22 each. How much did she spend all together?

> The phrase "a dozen pairs of socks" contains hidden information because **dozen** equals 12. Once you change the hidden information to a number, you can solve the problem.

Remember—

Problem solving has four steps:

1. **Read** the problem carefully to be sure you understand it.
2. **Plan** the steps you will take to find the answer.
3. **Solve** the problem using your plan.
4. **Check** your answer. Does it make sense?

"Missing" information is sometimes hidden in words. Change the hidden information into a number you can use.

1 dozen = 12
1 yard = 36 inches

4 quarters = $1.00

60 seconds = 1 minute
60 minutes = 1 hour
24 hours = 1 day

7 days = 1 week
12 months = 1 year
365 days = 1 year

Read each problem. Circle the letter of the best answer.

1 Cam drove from New York City to Hartford, Connecticut. The drive took about 3 hours, and the speed limit was 55 mph. What **more** do you need to know to find the distance traveled?

A how long Cam drove

B which road Cam took

C Cam's average speed

D how many gallons of gas he used

> Did you choose C? That's correct. Cam drove for 3 hours. To find the distance he traveled, you need to know his average speed.

2 Tami and her 2 friends spent 3 hours at the mall. They each spent $21.98 on DVDs. They also spent $8.99 on a pizza. What information is **not** needed to find the total the friends spent at the mall?

F They each spent $21.98 on DVDs.

G They spent 3 hours at the mall.

H Tami had 2 friends with her.

J They bought a pizza for $8.99.

3 It takes Mr. Musashi 20 minutes to shave and dress for work in the morning. What **other** information do you need to find how long it takes Mr. Musashi to shave?

A the time school starts

B the time his bus arrives

C the time he gets up in the morning

D the time it takes him to dress

Use this chart to answer questions 4–5.

Airport Limousine	One-Person Rates
Airport to Downtown	$35.00
Airport to Other Places	$10.00 + $5.00 per mile
Extra Person(s)	$5.00 for first
	$3.50 each additional
Bridge or tunnel tolls not included.	

4 Ms. Burk wants to go from the airport to her house, 4 miles away. What else does she need to know to find the total cost?

F the miles from the airport to downtown

G the bus fare to the airport

H the tolls from the airport to her house

J the time her plane gets in

5 Mr. Herrera and his family plan to go from the airport to downtown. What **other** information does he need in order to total his final cost for the ride?

A how many miles they will go

B where they went on their trip

C how many people are traveling

D when they are leaving

6 Erin began cleaning at 2:15 P.M. She went shopping from 4:15 to 5:30. At 6:30, she was done cleaning. Erin earns $6.50 per hour. What is **not** needed to figure out how much Erin earned to clean?

F She began cleaning at 2:15 P.M.

G She was done cleaning at 6:30.

H She went shopping from 4:15 to 5:30.

J She gets paid $6.50 per hour.

102

□ **Read each problem. Write your answer.**

Use this information to answer questions 7 and 8.

It takes Jane about $1\frac{1}{2}$ hours to deliver newspapers to the houses on her route, 6 days a week. Once a week, she collects $3.15 from each of her customers. The newspaper company gets $2.30 of each pay.

7 What *other* information is needed to find how much money Jane earns each week?

_____ **how many houses she delivers to on her route** _____

> Jane collects $3.15 from each customer per week and gives $2.30 to the company. So Jane gets $3.15 − $2.30, or $0.85 per customer. You need to know how many houses she delivers to on her route to figure out her total earnings.

8 What information is *not* needed to find Jane's earnings?

_____

Use this table to answer questions 9–11.

9 Diane took her car to Gary's Garage. She had an oil change and some tires repaired. What *other* information is needed to figure out the cost of the work?

_____

GARY'S GARAGE PRICE LIST	
Service	*Price in $*
Oil Change	24.50
Tire Repair (per tire)	10.00
Tune-up	35.00
Rotate tires	19.00

10 Fred brought his car to the garage to have the tires rotated and his engine tuned. Gary said it would take about $1\frac{1}{2}$ hours to do the job. What information is *not* needed to figure out Fred's bill?

_____

11 Megan took her car to the garage to have her tires rotated and a new muffler installed. Gary told her it would take about 1 hour. What *other* information do you need to figure out Megan's final cost?

_____

12 Martha took her niece and nephew to get ice cream.

Part A

Martha and her niece each ordered a large dish of chocolate with sprinkles. Her nephew ordered a small butter pecan in a pretzel cone. What **other** information do you need to find the total cost of their orders?

_____

Part B

Write a problem you could solve using the information in the chart.

_____

_____

_____

_____

_____

_____

Ask yourself—
What information has prices? What information does **not** have prices?

Before you write—
Think about the cost of each size of ice cream.

Now—
Check your answer. Does it make sense?

8–2 Non-Routine Problems

✸ Some problems take many steps to solve.

GREETING CARDS

1 Card
$2.25

Box of 10 Cards
$18.00

Curt needs to buy 20 greeting cards. How much money will Curt save by buying boxes of cards instead of 20 individual cards?

To solve this problem, find the value of 20 cards if they are bought separately:

20 × $2.25 = $45.00

Second, find how many boxes of cards are needed. Divide the total number of cards needed by the number of cards per box:

20 ÷ 10 = 2 boxes

Third, find the total price of the boxes of cards by multiplying:

2 × $18.00 = $36.00

Last, find the difference between the price of 20 individual cards and 20 cards in 2 boxes by subtracting:

$45.00 − $36.00 = $9.00

Curt would save $9.00 by buying 20 cards in 2 boxes.

Remember—

Non-routine problems may require you to use a formula, such as:

Area = Length × Width

Perimeter = (2 × length) × (2 × width)

Volume = length × width × height

Distance = rate × time

Rate is the speed units of distance: miles per hour, feet per second, etc.

Non-routine problems may have many parts and provide data in various forms, such as:
- Hidden information, such as coin values
- Measurements, such as time units
- Numbers in equivalent forms, such as fractions, decimals, or percents

Read each problem. Circle the letter of the best answer.

1 Gasoline costs $1.37 per gallon for regular and $1.52 per gallon for premium. How much less money would Winston have spent for 10 gallons of regular than premium?

  A $1.05   **C** $2.55

  B $1.50   **D** $15.20

> Did you pick B? That's correct. The difference in the price of a gallon is $0.15. The price difference for 10 gallons is 10 × $0.15 = $1.50, so he'd have spent $1.50 less.

Use this table to answer questions 2 and 3.

OAK SCHOOL'S PIZZA SALES	
Class	Amount Raised
Mr. Jones	$ 85
Mrs. Chan	$ 95
Mr. White	$ 70
Mrs. Popov	?
Ms. Verde	$102

2 All classes together raised $440. How much did Mrs. Popov's class raise?

  F $80   **H** $88

  G $86   **J** $94

3 What is the difference between the combined pizza sales of Mr. Jones and Ms. Verde's classes compared to Mrs. Chan's and Mr. White's?

  A $12   **C** $32

  B $22   **D** $42

4 Ethan set his watch to the exact time of 12 noon on Wednesday. At noon the next day, Ethan's watch read 11:58. How many seconds was Ethan's watch losing each hour?

  F 0.08 seconds   **H** 8.34 seconds

  G 5 seconds   **J** 10 seconds

Use this table to answer question 5.

TUESDAY'S BASKETBALL GAME		
Player	Points	Minutes
Keisha	17	38
Evelyn	15	44
Maria	24	37
Claire	11	41
Angie	9	24
Tabitha	16	8

5 Which player scored the most points per minutes played?

  A Maria   **C** Keisha

  B Tabitha   **D** Evelyn

6 Genevieve is thinking of two numbers. They have a sum of 17 and a product of 60. What is the larger number?

  F 5   **H** 10

  G 6   **J** 12

☐ **Read each problem. Write your answer.**

7 Andre made homemade candles in jars. He is stacking the candles in layers to fill the crate shown.

Each jar has a maximum width of 8 cm and is 12 cm tall. How many jars can Andre fit into the box without them sticking out the top?

_____45 jars_____

38 cm

40 cm

24 cm

> The bottom of the box is 24 cm × 40 cm. Divide to find how many 8 cm jars will fit across the box and how many will fit from to back: 24 ÷ 8 = 3 jars across, 40 ÷ 8 = 5 jars front to back. That means 3 × 5, or 15 jars can fit in 1 layer. The height, 38 cm, can hold 3 layers of jars: 38 ÷ 12 = 3R2. Since no jars may stick up over the top edge, 3 × 15, or 45 jars will fit in the box.

Use this menu to answer questions 8–9.

8 The Anderson family stopped at the drive-through window and ordered 5 tacos, 3 beef burritos, and 4 chicken and cheese quesadillas. What was their total bill? Show your work.

_____

DOLLY'S TAMALES MENU	
Taco (hard or soft)	$0.79
6-pack	$4.25
Burrito (bean)	$1.69
Burrito (beef)	$1.89
Quesadilla (cheese only)	$1.29
Quesadilla (cheese + chicken)	$1.59
Nachos Supremos	$3.29
Drinks (unlimited refills)	$1.05

9 Wakan wants 5 tacos, Jocelyn wants 4 tacos, and Willy wants 3. How much money would the 3 friends save by putting their orders together and buying 6-packs? Show your work.

_____

10 The diagram shows a rectangular patio. Aida wants to cover the patio with paving stones. Each stone is 3 feet long and 1 foot wide. How many stones will it take to cover the patio? Show your work.

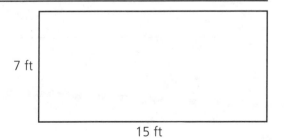

7 ft

15 ft

_____

11 The McAfee family left on a camping trip with a full 20 gallons of gas. The first day, they traveled 150 miles and visited with Aunt Lois. They stayed over at her house. The next morning, they drove 120 miles before stopping for lunch and filling the gas tank with 15 gallons. They drove 144 miles that afternoon, and reached the campground before dark.

Part A

If the family used gas at the same rate, how much gas was left in the tank when they reached the campground? Show your work.

Part B

The family drove the same route home. At $1.38 a gallon, how much did they spend on gas to get home? Explain how you found your answer.

Ask yourself—
How many miles did the family travel in total? How many gallons of gas did they purchase during the trip?

Before you write—
Think about how many miles per gallon the McAfee's family car averaged.

Now—
Check your answer. Does it make sense?

8–R Problem Solving and Reasoning Review

Read each problem. Circle the letter of the best answer.

1 Shawn walks his neighbor's dog on weekdays and gets $2.50 per walk. What **other** information is needed to find how much Shawn earned in one week?

   A how far Shawn walked the dog

   B how long Shawn walked the dog

   C how often Shawn walked the dog

   D how well Shawn took care of the dog

Use this table to answer questions 2 and 3.

BUTTER PRICES

Month	May	June	July
Cost Per Pound	$1.99	$2.39	$2.89

2 Steph bought 5 pounds of butter in July. How much less did it cost her to buy the same amount in May?

   F $0.90   **H** $2.50

   G $2.00   **J** $4.50

3 What is the average cost of a pound of butter?

   A $2.00   **C** $2.42

   B $2.19   **D** $2.64

4 Plain pizza slices cost $1.25. Onion slices cost $1.75. Drinks are $1.05. Sal ordered 2 slices and a drink. What else do you need to find the total Sal spent?

   F the kind of drink he bought

   G the kind of slices he bought

   H whether he had pizza left over

   J whether he ate in or took it out

Use this drawing to answer questions 5 and 6.

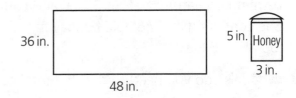

5 How many jars of honey will fit standing upright in a single layer on this table?

   A 12   **C** 208

   B 16   **D** 576

6 Which piece of data in the diagram is **not** needed?

   F 3 in.   **H** 36 in.

   G 5 in.   **J** 48 in.

Use this table to answer questions 7 and 8.

PETS OWNED

Type of Pet	Dog	Cat	Bird
Number Owned	18	23	7

7 What fraction of the pets are cats or birds?

   A $\frac{3}{5}$ **C** $\frac{3}{8}$

   B $\frac{5}{6}$ **D** $\frac{5}{8}$

8 What question **cannot** be answered using the information in the table?

   F How many students own pets?

   G How many more dogs are owned than cats?

   H How many birds and cats are owned together?

   J How many students own more than one pet?

Use this information to answer questions 9 and 10.

Jennifer used 3 gallons of paint to paint a fence. She began painting on Saturday at 8:15 A.M. and continued until 5:30 P.M. She continued at 7:45 A.M. Sunday morning and completed the job at 3:30 P.M.

Deck & Fence Paint

9 What else do you need to find the total cost of the paint?

_____

10 How long did it take Jennifer to complete the job? Show your work.

_____

_____

11 What **other** information is needed to find the difference in area between Palmer Park and Arnold Park?

280 yd — Palmer Park

Arnold Park — 160 yd

360 yd

_____

■ **Read the problem. Write your answer for each part.**

12 Kevin has to bring sodas to a party for 30 people.

Part A

How much will it cost Kevin to buy 30 sodas in packs of 6? Show your work.

6 Sodas
$2.89

10 cans

10 Sodas
$4.99

_____

Part B

Does it cost less to buy 30 sodas in packs of 6 or boxes of 10? Explain how you found your answer.

_____

_____

110